40269

Warner, Alan
William Allingham

William Allingham

THE IRISH WRITERS SERIES
James F. Carens, General Editor

EIMAR O'DUFFY	Robert Hogan
J. C. MANGAN	James Kilroy
J. M. SYNGE	Robin Skelton
PAUL VINCENT CARROLL	Paul A. Doyle
SEAN O'CASEY	Bernard Benstock
SEUMAS O'KELLY	George Brandon Saul
SHERIDAN LEFANU	Michael Begnal
SOMERVILLE AND ROSS	John Cronin
STANDISH O'GRADY	Phillip L. Marcus
SUSAN L. MITCHELL	Richard M. Kain
W. R. RODGERS	Darcy O'Brien
MERVYN WALL	Robert Hogan
LADY GREGORY	Hazard Adams
LIAM O'FLAHERTY	James O'Brien
MARIA EDGEWORTH	James Newcomer
SIR SAMUEL FERGUSON	Malcolm Brown
BRIAN FRIEL	D. E. S. Maxwell
PEADAR O'DONNELL	Grattan Freyer
DANIEL CORKERY	George Brandon Saul
BENEDICT KIELY	Daniel Casey
CHARLES ROBERT MATURIN	Robert E. Lougy
DOUGLAS HYDE	Gareth Dunleavy
EDNA O'BRIEN	Grace Eckley
FRANCIS STUART	J. H. Natterstad
JOHN BUTLER YEATS	Douglas N. Archibald
JOHN MONTAGUE	Frank Kersnowski
KATHARINE TYNAN	Marilyn Gaddis Rose
BRIAN MOORE	Jeanne Flood
PATRICK KAVANAGH	Darcy O'Brien
OLIVER ST. JOHN GOGARTY	J. B. Lyons
GEORGE FITZMAURICE	Arthur McGuinness

GEORGE RUSSELL (AE)	Richard M. Kain and James H. O'Brien
IRIS MURDOCH	Donna Gerstenberger
MARY LAVIN	Zack Bowen
FRANK O'CONNOR	James H. Matthews
ELIZABETH BOWEN	Edwin J. Kenney, Jr.
WILLIAM ALLINGHAM	Alan Warner
SEAMUS HEANEY	Robert Buttel
THOMAS DAVIS	Eileen Sullivan

WILLIAM ALLINGHAM

Alan Warner

Lewisburg
BUCKNELL UNIVERSITY PRESS
London: ASSOCIATED UNIVERSITY PRESSES

©1975 by Associated University Presses, Inc.

Associated University Presses, Inc.
Cranbury, New Jersey 08512

Associated University Presses
108 New Bond Street
London W1Y OQX, England

Library of Congress Cataloging in Publication Data
Warner, Alan, 1912–
    William Allingham.

    (The Irish writers series)
    Bibliography: p.
    1. Allingham, William, 1824-1889–Criticism and
interpretation.
PR4004.A5W29   821'.8   79-168822
ISBN 0-8387-7899-2
ISBN 0-8387-7990-5 pbk.

Contents

Introduction

W. B. Yeats always considered William Allingham as one of his predecessors who had worked toward a tradition of Irish writing in English. In December, 1904, he wrote to Mrs. Allingham, the poet's widow, asking permission to publish a selection of her husband's poems in a series from the Dun Emer Press:

> Books by AE, by Lionel Johnson, by Douglas Hyde and by myself have already been printed and a book by Lady Gregory will follow the selection of your husband's poems should you give me permission. We are anxious to bring out in this series representative Irish books. I have the greatest possible admiration for Mr. Allingham's poetry. I am sometimes inclined to believe that he was my own master in Irish verse, starting me in the way I have gone whether for good or evil. I believe that I shall be able to make a little volume of his work which will be a great joy to a great many people.

Long before this, when Yeats was reviewing the six-volume collected edition of Allingham's poems in *United Ireland* (December 12, 1891) he had added him to the holy trinity of Davis, Mangan, and Ferguson. "It is time for us over here to claim him as our own, and give him his due place among our sacred poets; to range his books beside Davis and Mangan and Ferguson; for he, too, sang of Irish scenes and Irish faces."

Katharine Tynan also placed Allingham in the Irish tradition, finding in his poetry "keen sympathy and understanding", an expression of "the Irish spirit." Amongst other Irish men of letters who gave high praise to Allingham's poetry were Lionel Johnson, A.P. Graves, and Geoffrey Taylor. The latter did not share Katharine Tynan's conviction that he was unmistakably Irish of the Irish, but he still considered him "among the very best of Anglo-Irish poets."

It was not only Irish men of letters who appreciated Allingham. In England he had many admirers amongst the foremost writers of his time. Tennyson, Browning, Rossetti, Dickens, and Coventry Patmore all praised him. But in spite of this he has had few readers. He was not passionate or national enough to make an impact on Irish readers, while English readers were not really interested in poems about Ireland. As Lionel Johnson noted, in his fame and in his life Allingham remains a rather lonely figure. Although he was intimate with D.G. Rossetti for many years and he moved freely in the Pre-Raphaelite group of painters and poets, he was never one of them. Nor did he belong to any Irish group, though he was friendly with Samuel Ferguson.

Allingham's claim to our attention today rests on a real achievement in three fields. First there is his long narrative poem on the Irish land troubles of the eighteen-sixties, *Laurence Bloomfield in Ireland.* Geoffrey Taylor rightly claims "that it is, judged by European standards, a minor classic." It gave Turgenev an insight into Ireland; Gladstone praised it and quoted from it in the House of Commons.

Second—many critics would put it first—there is Allingham's achievement as a lyric poet, as a writer of ballads and songs. His best ballads belong to a folk tradition. He was himself a connoiseur and collector, and he heard ballads sung at the fairs in Ballyshannon. He collected airs and wrote them down; many of his own ballads are set to popular airs. He also wrote a number of more personal lyrics. Although his songs for children are probably the best known and most anthologized of all his writings—songs such as "The Fairies", "Robin Redbreast", "Wishing", and "The Leprechaun"—his more personal lyrics are his best. Many of these have not only a musical charm and sweetness, but they subtly evoke moods and feelings that lie deeper than charm.

Third, Allingham wrote a good deal of prose that shows real powers of observation, imagination, and reflection. Foremost is his *Diary,* which reveals something of Boswell's sharp eye and ear for detail. He also published a series of *Rambles* under the pseudonym of Patricius Walker in 1873. Always a keen walker and a devoted literary pilgrim, he rambled in the southern counties of England, in Scotland, and in France. Perhaps his most interesting observations are to be found in his "Irish Sketches". His account of Irish ballad singers and street ballads is full of interest; and he records folk-customs and traditional celebrations with an accurate and sympathetic eye. He was one of the few outsiders to visit St. Patrick's Purgatory, and offers us "perhaps the only account in existence of this famous place in station-time, by a non-pilgrim eye-witness."

Allingham also wrote a number of biographical and critical essays, and for a time he contributed a personal column to *Fraser's.* He was an indefatigable letterwriter, writing to Leigh Hunt, Emerson, Carlyle, D.G. Rossetti, Arthur Hughes, Henry Sutton, the Burne-Joneses, the Brownings, the Fergusons, and many others. Relatively few of his letters have survived, but there are enough to show that he could be a lively and engaging correspondent.

It will be clear from this brief account of his work that Allingham is much more than the author of a few memorable lyrics and ballads. It is surprising that no full-length study of the man or his work has yet appeared in print. Perhaps it is because there is nothing dramatic or obviously newsworthy in his life or writings that he has so far found relatively few readers. Until very recently most of his work was out of print. Yet he deserves an honorable place in the ranks of Irish writers. "I am genuine though not great," he wrote to Thomas Woolner, "and my turn will come."

My own opportunity to read and write about William Allingham has been largely due to my tenure of the Hugh le May Fellowship at Rhodes University, Grahamstown, South Africa. I wish to record my sincere gratitude to this university.

Chronology

1824   Born in Ballyshannon, Co. Donegal.

1838   Leaves school to work in the local bank.

1843   Begins a correspondence with Leigh Hunt.

1846   Enters Customs service and becomes Principal Coast Officer stationed in Donegal town.

1847   Meets Leigh Hunt on a holiday visit to London. Writes to R. W. Emerson, who was on a visit to England, and a brief exchange of letters begins.

1848   Meets Coventry Patmore.

1850   *Poems* published with a dedication to Leigh Hunt. Sees much of the Pre-Raphaelite group on his annual summer holiday in London.

1851   First meeting with Tennyson at Twickenham.

1853   Transferred to Coleraine Customs, Co. Londonderry.

1854   Resigns from the Customs to try a literary life in London but after a few months decides to return to the Customs.
        Day and Night Songs.

1855   *The Music Master* and Two Series of Day and Night songs.

1860   *Nightingale Valley.*

1861   *Poems* published in Boston.
1862   Exchanges his post in Ballyshannon for one in the London docks; becomes ill and later returns to Ballyshannon.
1863   Makes another exchange within the Customs to Lyminton in Hampshire. This time he remains in England for good.
1864   *Laurence Bloomfield in Ireland.*
        The Ballad Book.
        Awarded a Civil List pension of £60 a year on the recommendation of Lord Palmerston.
1865   *Fifty Modern Poems.*
1866   His father dies in Ballyshannon. Last visit to Ireland.
1870   Gives up Customs post at Lymington to become subeditor of *Fraser's* magazine.
1873   *Rambles* by "Patricius Walker".
1874   Becomes editor of *Fraser's* magazine succeeding J.A. Froude. Marries Helen Paterson, water-color painter.
1875   Birth of first child, Gerald Carlyle.
1877   *Songs, Ballads and Stories.*
        Birth of second child, Eva Margaret.
1881   Death of Carlyle. The Allinghams move to Witley in Surrey.
1882   *Evil May-Day.*
        Birth of third child, Henry William.
1883   *Ashby Manor* (a play in two acts).
1884   *Blackberries.*
1887   *Irish Songs and Poems.*
1888   The Allinghams move from Surrey to Hampstead.

1889   *Life and Phantasy.*
Dies and is cremated at Woking cemetery. His ashes buried in St. Anne's churchyard at Bally-shannon.

William Allingham

1

The Poet of Ballyshannon

This was the title that Yeats used when he wrote an article on Allingham for the *Providence Sunday Journal.* Katharine Tynan sent a copy of the article to Allingham and he noted in his diary—"non-national, how sad!" I shall be discussing in the last chapter how far Allingham may be considered a national poet, but certainly his roots, both as man and poet, are in Ballyshannon.

Ballyshannon, a small market town in the southwest corner of Co. Donegal, straddles the river Erne where it runs into the Atlantic. At one time an important gateway into Ulster, the frontier town of ancient Tirconnail, by the beginning of the nineteenth century it was in a state of gentle decline. It was a port, but the harbor was not large or deep enough for the big vessels that were to develop in the nineteenth century. Several units of the British army had occupied barracks in Ballyshannon but as the years passed they were withdrawn, first the cavalry, then the artillery and finally the red-coated infantry that impressed Allingham as a boy. But the town was picturesque and had a distinctive character:

The little town where I was born has a Voice of its own, low, solemn, persistent, humming through the air day and night, summer and winter. Whenever I think of that Town I seem to hear the Voice. The River, which makes it, rolls over rocky ledges into the tide; before spreads a great ocean in sunshine or storm; behind stretches a many-islanded Lake. On the south runs a wavy line of blue mountains and to the north over green or rocky hills rise peaks of a more distant range.

The genesis of Allingham's poetry was in Ballyshannon, as he freely confessed. Two years before he died he published a selection, entitled *Irish Songs and Poems,* and in the preface he states: "By a certain River, with its harbour and bay, lies the native region of most of these poems."

Allingham's life can be clearly divided into two halves—the Irish half and the English half. From his birth in 1824 until 1863 he lived in Ireland, mostly in Ballyshannon itself. From 1863 (when he moved from the Irish Customs service to a post as Customs Officer at Lymington, Hampshire), until his death in Hampstead in 1889, he lived in England. But it would be wrong to make too sharp a division between the Irish and English periods of his life. In Ballyshannon his eyes were often turned towards England; he frequently visited London during his holidays and his correspondents were mainly English. In England he seriously contemplated writing a history of Ireland; he did in fact contribute some Irish papers to *Fraser's;* and his thoughts often turned to Ireland. After a social evening in London he notes in his diary "Home: stars (I think of Ballyshannon and the sound of the Atlantic)."

Allingham's ancestors migrated from England in the time of Queen Elizabeth I and settled in Ballyshannon. They became part of the local Protestant ascendancy and were comfortably off, though not rich. The poet's father, also William Allingham, was a merchant and importer. He became manager of the local branch of the Provincial Bank, where his son was later to begin work reluctantly at the age of fourteen. The elder Allingham removed his son from school because his doctor warned him that he might not have long to live, and he wished his son to be self-supporting. In the event the father lived until 1866, but the son continued to work, first in various branches of the bank, and then in the Customs service. So Allingham was by no means a scion of the Big House. Nor did he shoot and fish or ride to hounds. By temperament he was averse to blood-sports. His recreations were walking, music, and reading, and later, of course, poetry. But although he was not in the tradition of the Big House, and despite the fact that he remained poor most of his life, Allingham was by birth and background a "gentleman", inevitably separated from the local peasantry. One of the first of his poems to attract attention was "The Pilot's Daughter". In it he described his meeting, on a balmy spring evening, with the charming daughter of the local fisherman-pilot. Her native Irish charm is enhanced by a neat Sunday frock, a modest blush and the clear cadence of her voice, so that the poet dreams of sharing a cottage home with her:

> Were it my lot, there peeped a wish,
>   To hand a pilot's oar and sail,
> Or haul the dripping moonlight mesh,

> Spangled with herring-scale;
> By dying stars, how sweet 'twould be,
> And dawn-blow freshening the sea,
> With weary, cheery pull to shore,
> To gain my cottage home once more,
> And meet, before I reached the door
>   My darling Pilot's Daughter!

But the poet recognizes that his wish is no more than a passing dream. The gulf between himself and the "Poor" is too wide to bridge. He reminds himself of the harsh reality of life in, "A fisher's hut, the scene perforce/ Of narrow thoughts and manners coarse. . . ." As to the possiblity of raising *her* to his level, it is wiser to let such thoughts alone. The poem ends with the poet's resolve to admire the beauty of the "simple maid" as he admires the stars.

Though Allingham remains a detached spectator of the peasant world around him, he knew it well, and "Master Willy", (the name he was generally known by) was a welcome visitor to farm and cottage for many miles around Ballyshannon. Here were the scenes and the people that figured in his earliest writings, and he consciously attempted to depict the local scene. He confided his ambition to Emerson in an early letter, written in December, 1847, "to try something like Irish Idyls— but not to be efforts at Irishism, but at Nature with the (necessary) local colouring."

In fact the local coloring is spread somewhat thinly in Allingham's first volume (*Poems,* 1850). Some of the poems had nothing at all to do with the world he was living in; their inspiration was purely literary. Such are the two "Valentines", most of his poems on love and the fanciful series on poets and flowers, in which he matches the English poets with appropriate flowers; hyacinth for Keats, buttercup for Clare, and so on. These verses are indeed what Professor Doughty once called "smooth insipidities".

Even when Allingham is writing of nature it is often a literary, unlocalized nature. It must be frankly admitted that the reader who tackles the poems in bulk has a good deal of trite and facile versing to put aside before he comes to the more rewarding poems. "The Wayside Well" is an example:

> O thou pretty wayside well
>   Wreathed about with roses,
> Where, beguiled with soothing spell,
>   Weary foot reposes.

Allingham naturally does his best work when his own feelings are involved in the local scene. In "A Burial Place" he is thinking of his own death and he describes vividly and accurately the river and harbor that he knew and loved:

> The silver salmon shooting up the fall
>   Itself at once the arrow and the bow;
> The shadow of the old quay's weedy wall
>   Cast on the shining turbulence below;
> The water-voice which ever seemed to call
>   Far-off out of my childhood's long-ago;
> The gentle washing of the harbour wave;
> Be these the sounds and sights around my grave.

There is no doubt about the local coloring in this poem; it is clearly set in Ballyshannon, and the same is true of the next untitled poem, which has only two verses. It is easy to imagine Allingham walking lonely by the river in the late evening and longing for that "not impossible she", that beloved companion, who was not to come to his side until his fiftieth year:

> The mild promising stars are coming into view,
>   The voice of the waterfall is toning in the air,
>   Whilst lazily the cloud-fire smoulders on the sea
> And all the landscape-outlines are blurred with
>   falling dew,—
>   As my rapture is with sadness, because I may not share,
>   And double it by sharing it with Thee.
>
> Now the calm shadowy earth lies musing like a saint,
>   Wearing for a halo the pure circlet of the moon;
>   Like a full happy heart is the flowing of the tide;
> And the night-wind from the mountain breathes steady,
>   though so faint,—
>   As I am breathing softly, "Ah! might some heavenly
>   boon
>   Bestow thee, my beloved one, to my side!"

There is a subtler rhythm in these lines than in many of Allingham's lyrics, and the melancholy has a tender, reflective note that might be called distinctively Irish. When Katharine Tynan attempted to define "the Irish note" in her essay on Allingham, she became delightfully vague and all-embracing, but she included in her broad net "a shade of underlying melancholy as delicately evanescent as a breath upon glass, which yet gives its undertone and its shadow to all." Certainly this undertone and shadow are found in nearly all the better poems in Allingham's first volume. To those I have already mentioned could be added "The Dream", The Ruined Chapel", and "Sweet Sunday Bells". In none of these poems is there any strong feeling of local landscape, though they all belong to Ballyshannon; but because they spring from a personal and not a literary inspiration the musical movement of the lines is not simply facile; it has a haunting poignancy that is Allingham at his lyrical best. "The Dream" is a dream of the dead and it has the force of a real dream:

> I heard the dogs howl in the moonlight night;
> I went to the window to see the sight;
> All the Dead that ever I knew
> Going one by one and two by two.
>
> On they passed, and on they passed;
> Townsfellows all from first to last;
> Born in the moonlight of the lane
> Quenched in the heavy shadow again.

Only one of the "long, long crowd", looks at the poet-his mother, long since dead. The poem trembles on the edge of conventional sentiment but sweeps us on "Across the moon-stream, from shade to shade." The sense of being haunted by a dream is caught in the cadence as well as in the mood of the poem. It is a mood and a mode that was to be echoed frequently by Yeats in his early poems.

"Sweet Sunday Bells" is simple almost to the point of naivety. The church bells, the familiar voice of Sunday peace, bring a pleasure mixed with sadness to the poet. Allingham could not accept the theology of the Anglican church to which all his people belonged, nor any other dogmatic theology. As he listens to the bells he is aware of his position outside the traditional fold as one,—

> Whose heart to your old music swells;
> Whose soul a deeper thought impels
> Who like an alien sadly dwells
> Within your chime—sweet Sunday Bells.

The single rhyme, repeated through each stanza, carries

a faint suggestion of the ringing bells. The lines seem to be moving to a climax, only to fall sadly away at the end.

There are perhaps a dozen lyrics in Allingham's first volume that are worth preserving, including the popular child's song, "The Fairies", which also left its echoes in the early poetry of Yeats; but the rest is mainly literary "versing" that is best forgotten. There remains "The Music Master", a long narrative poem, the nearest thing perhaps to an "Irish Idyll" in the book.

"The Music Master" received high praise from many people when it appeared, and Allingham reprinted it in a revised form in 1855. An early reviewer wrote rapturously of its "genuine poetry of the affections, tenderness, sensibility, delicacy, simplicity and truth." "The Music Master" is not without merit in detail. It contains some of the best of Allingham's descriptive writing but the story is feeble in the extreme, appealling to the worst side of sentimental Victorian taste. Claude, a young music teacher and the local organist, falls in love with one of his pupils, Milly, who lives in a secluded cottage on the bank of the river. The lovers walk and talk together in the summer evenings but are too shy and diffident to declare their love. Then one evening Claude, arriving early at the cottage, plays the piano, and expresses his unspoken love in his playing so clearly that Milly, listening, and weeping, unobserved, is about to step forward and their love will be plainly acknowledged. But she is interrupted by the alien voice of her mean-spirited sister Ann. She turns away, Claude goes home to find his father dead. Soon afterwards his uncle from America suggests that he too should emigrate to the West and he agrees. There is a brief parting scene at the cottage and love remains unacknowledged.

Part II of the poem tells how five years later Claude returns to his home village and visits first his parents' graves, then Milly's. She had died at the age of eighteen. The poem is not very clear about the cause of her death; presumably her gentle wasting malady was aggravated by a broken heart. At the graveside Claude meets Milly's old gray-haired nurse, who tells him that Milly on her death bed had confessed her love for Claude and left in the nurse's care a parcel for him. Alone in his room that evening, Claude opens the parcel, which contains Milly's portrait, a lock of her hair and a farewell note. Claude returns to America and years afterwards a letter brings news of him to the village. Some of his compatriots had stumbled upon him where he lived alone in the American woods.

> One spoke about a wife
> To cheer him in that solitary wild;
> At which he only shook his head and smiled.

The poem ends as they leave him next morning to his music and his memories.

I think Allingham admires, and intends his readers to admire, the pure, long-suffering, spiritual love of Claude and Milly, who accept parting and death with humble resignation to "His Will" who "said no," and "who orders all things for the best." D.G. Rossetti who was a good deal impressed by the poem wrote to Allingham: "The Music Master" is full of beauty and nobility, but I'm not sure it is not *too* noble or too resolutely healthy."

Rossetti is right. The whole thing is much too noble to be true, if "noble" is the right word. As for its healthiness, so much abnegation is decidedly unhealthy. One finds oneself wishing that Milly or Claude would cry out against God and the injustice of events. The lovers are not heroic but simply stupid. Why does Claude not find a way to declare his love? His silent worship is not pure and noble but simply a lack of courage and initiative. Shakespeare would have laughed at such a version of Romeo and Juliet. Is there perhaps at a subconscious level in Allingham's mind a desire to let love be a dream rather than a fleshly reality? When Claude finally falls asleep on the restless night that follows his opening of Milly's parcel he is visited with a beautiful dream of heavenly happiness: "And thither through the soft air glided they,/ Himself and Milly."

For all the weakness of the story there is such vivid descriptive detail in the poem that the reader reads on; the story is not so much dull as unacceptable. One of the best passages in the poem describes the sleepy village, "lazied in dusty sunshine," when Claude returns to it:

> Each hollyhock within its little wall
>   Sleeps in the richness of its crusted blooms;
> Up the hot glass the sluggish blue flies crawl;
>   The heavy bee is humming into rooms
> Through open window, like a sturdy rover,
> Bringing with him warm scents of thyme and clover.
>
> From little cottage-gardens you almost
>   Smell the fruit ripening on the sultry air;
> Opprest to silence, every bird is lost
>   In eave and hedgerow; save that here and there
> With twitter soft, the sole unquiet thing,
> Shoots the dark lightning of a swallow's wing.

The sense of a drowsy summer day is finely caught here and the last line contains a flash of vivid and original imagery such as Allingham rarely rises to.

The detail of the natural description in the poem, of street, garden, river bank and churchyard, is clearly based on Ballyshannon, and yet most of the description could apply almost equally well to an English village and landscape. In his "Familiar Epistle to a Little Boy", Allingham speaks of his birthplace, "On that wild verge of Europe, in dark Donegal." But the more dramatic aspects of the Donegal landscape, the harsh and desolate grandeur of bog and mountain, are found very rarely in his poetry; though his prose shows clearly enough that he was observant of these aspects. In his *Diary* there is an account of a journey from Donegal to Ardara:

> Outside car, moors and bare mountains to Ardara, when the groves of Woodhill give a softening. The sun set into a jagged cloud breaking flame from its openings, rested on the dark mountains, disappeared, leaving a gloomy memory which soon faded too. Then the wind blew colder, the road became indistinct, the moors blended into a dim waste.

Claude's return could equally well have been imagined against a background such as this. Did the example of English poets, of Tennyson in particular, influence Allingham toward the more conventional pastoral moods that chiefly figure in his poetry?

Certainly if we take the *Poems* as a whole, we must admit that the landscape and the moods owe more to literature than to the real people and places of "dark Donegal", in spite of references to Ballyshannon. We are aware of Allingham's anxious labouring to succeed as a poet, to enter the world of literature, but we become aware that he lacks a central creative impulse and this lack is what keeps him a minor writer. With the possible exception of *Laurence Bloomfield in Ireland,* we cannot feel of any of his work that he was compelled to utterance by a passion and intensity of feeling that would not be denied. But after his first volume he moved in two different directions that gave him an increase of strength and force. First, he moved towards folk music and the traditional ballad, and over the next ten years he wrote a number of successful ballads. Second, he used verse to make social and political comment, notably in *Laurence Bloomfield in Ireland.*

2

Ballads and Songs

Allingham had always had an alert and sympathetic ear for the ballads and songs that he heard sung in and around Ballyshannon. In "The Music Master" he records how as "a friendly spy" he went strolling past houses and cottages, listening to flute or fiddle or song. Years later, at a performance of *Arrah-na-Pogue* in London he was melted by Boucicault's singing of "The Wearing of the Green", "which I hear was prohibited by the authorities in Dublin on account of the wild excitement it caused in the theatre."

Allingham was a keen student of ballads in general and he compiled an anthology of "the choicest British ballads", which was published by Macmillan in their Golden Treasury Series in 1864. In the preface to *The Ballad Book,* as it was called, he tells us that "moved by a natural affection for ballads," he "not only made himself acquainted with all ballads and ballad literature that came within his reach, but might perhaps, if he chose, set up some claim to be considered as an original collector in a small way—Ireland being his principal field."

Regretting that Ireland's native popular songs and ballads lie hid in Gaelic, he nevertheless noted that "Many of the English and Scottish ballads, however, were carried over to the neighbouring island, and are still borne in the memory of humble people. . ."

He claimed too that he had "also a large collection of the ballads and songs, printed on slips of whitey-brown paper, sold by hawkers and professional ballad-singers throughout Ireland at the present day. . ."

Much earlier, in 1852, Allingham had contributed an interesting essay to *Household Words* on "Irish Ballad Singers and Irish Street Ballads". He describes the scene on Fair-day in Ballyshannon.

> At our elbow a ballad-singer, a young woman in old plaid cloak and very old straw bonnet, strikes up, with a sweet Connaught lisp, and slightly nasal twang, "The Sorrowful Lamentations of Patrick Donohoe"—with the words, "Come all you tender Christians!"—and soon summons around her a ring of listeners. She will sing *da capo* as long as the ballad appears to draw attention and custom, and then she will change it or move off to another part of the fair.

He describes his own collection of broadside ballads "printed on gray paper with coarse type", headed with most incompatible woodcuts, and filled with every kind of typographical error; and in his essay he provides an interesting commentary on their subject matter and style, with numerous examples.

He tried the experiment of issuing some of his own ballads as broadside. He tells us in the preface to his next volume of poems, *The Music Master and two series of day and night songs* (1855) that five of the songs or ballads had already had an Irish circulation as "ha'penny ballads". In a letter to Mr. and Mrs. Robert Browning, written from Coleraine, Co. Londonderry, he writes:

I have contributed half-a-dozen songs to the stock of one of the Dublin ballad printers, and send you one [Mary Donnelly].
The printer told me that when there were a dozen or so of my songs he would print them in a little book. "Price a penny?" "Why, Sir, it's not everyone buys a penny book—but a ha'penny book is sure to sell." To be sure to sell, at any price, is truly delightful.

Allingham never did in fact make up a little book of songs to be sold for a ha'penny, but he did have a number printed on broadsheets. Unfortunately very few of these broadsheets have survived, but there are one or two in the ballad collection of Trinity College, Dublin, where one narrow sheet contains 'Kitty O'Hay' and "Lovely Mary Donnelly' side by side, with a woodcut in the lefthand top corner.

One result of Allingham's venture into the broadside ballad market was that he heard his own songs sung in the streets and cottages by people who were quite unconscious of his authorship. In a letter to Henry Sutton, 17 June, 1852, he wrote:

I have for some part of my verses a little audience such as few poets can boast of, to whom Tennyson would, likely, seem to be the name of a town.

The enclosed song of 'The Milkmaid' I heard sung at a cottage door (to be truthful I ought to say "hovel door") by a chorus of 6 or 8 girls and boys.

A few years later when he was writing to Mrs. Taylor, with whom he often stayed in London, he added a postscript: "I enclose a local ballad of mine which has been sung in the street here. One day, finishing a letter for a woman to her daughter in America, I said "Is there anything more?" On which she pulled out a crumpled copy of the ballad. "Aye, we'll send her this, and it might make her come home." I should have said that the letter was an entreaty to her daughter to return." The ballad must have been "The Winding Banks of Erne."

Although Allingham did not write more than a dozen "broadside" ballads he pioneered a mode that was later to be taken up by several writers of the Irish literary revival, such as Yeats, Colum, and Joseph Campbell. His own ballads have considerable liveliness and force; the folk tradition of the ballad with its frankness and vigor was a better influence on Allingham than the prevailing modes of Victorian "poesy". "The Girl's Lamentation", for example, although the subject is old and time-worn, succeeds in conveying a real compassion for human distress. This is one of the poems Allingham wrote expressly for broadside circulation. It incorporates many familiar ballad lines—"For a maid again I can never be Till the red rose blooms on the willow tree"— but Allingham gives it his own shape and tone, and he adds details of his own. I have not met elsewhere the reference to Candlemas crosses that he makes use of:

> The Candlemas crosses hang near my bed;
> To look on them puts me much in dread,
> They mark the good time that's gone and past:
> It's like this year's one will prove the last.
>
> The oldest cross it's a dusty brown,
> But the winter winds didn't shake it down;

The newest cross keeps the colour bright,—
When the straw was reaping my heart was light.

The reapers rose with the blink of morn,
And gaily stook'd up the yellow corn,
To call them home to the field I'd run,
Through the blowing breeze and the summer sun.

For their full effect, of course, these ballads should be
sung. Allingham wrote the words with a traditional tune
sounding in his head. He tells us in his preface that"
"The Nobleman's Wedding" is moulded out of a frag-
mentary ditty sung by an old nurse who was in the family of my respected friend Dr. Petrie, to an air which he
intends to include in his collection of Melodies. . ."
"Lovely Mary Donnelly" clearly calls out for a dancing
measure:

When she stood up for dancing, her steps were so complete
The music nearly kill'd itself to listen to her feet;
The fiddler moaned his blindness, he heard her so much
                                    praised,
But bless'd his luck to be not deaf when once her voice
                                    she raised.

Although Allingham wrote only about ten popular
broadside ballads there is a good deal of variety in them,
and one wishes he had done more in this mode, and less
in the more literary mode of "Lady Alice." One wishes
also that he had been less conventional and conservative
in his approach to the language of the ballads. In the
preface to *The Music Master,* he explains that he avoids
dialect because "that phraseology, being as regards its
structural peculiarities but an imperfect or distorted
expression, not an ancient dialect like that of Scotland,
is generally too corrupt (though often forcible) to bear

transplantation into poetry..." And apparently he believed "that the choice of words for poetry in Irish-English is narrowly limited, instead of there being that accession both of variety and raciness which is sometimes in the gift of a genuine peculiar dialect." The difficulties are real ones. None of the nineteenth-century Irish poets was able to make any effective use of the Anglo-Irish idiom in his poetry, and even Synge was to develop it in prose not verse. But Allingham admired William Barnes's Dorset poems, and introduced them to Tennyson and other friends. We even find him experimenting with the Warwickshire dialect in his poem on "Old Master Grunsey and Goodman Dodd," though this remains a dull and rather obviously contrived poem. Had Allingham shown less respect for "the laws of poetic taste and the rules of grammar," he might have felt freer to make use of local idioms, and he might have gone further with broadside ballads.

Naturally enough Allingham tried his hand at literary ballads too, in the mode of the romantic poets. "The Abbot of Inisfalen" is perhaps his best. It tells the story of a Killarney legend about a Rip van Winkle of the cloister. The Abbot went out one morning and followed a little white singing bird; when he returned to the Abbey two hundred years had passed. Allingham tells the story in a simple, repetitive ballad style that moves with speed and is not without a certain dramatic power. There is dramatic power also, in the more lurid story told in "The Ballad of Squire Curtis," despite the unnecessary distraction of a narrator with the mildly comic name of Henry Dabb. The story tells of a cruel squire who murdered his young wife and buried her in a dark wood. When he returns home he finds that she has preceded him, as her waiting woman reports:

"Her face was white as any corpse
  As up the stair she pass'd;
She never turned, she never spoke;
  And the chamber-door is fast.

"She's waiting for you." "A lie!" he shouts,
  And up to his feet doth start;
"My wife is buried in Brimley Holt,
  With three wounds in her heart."

A literary ballad in a more Pre-Raphaelite mode is "The Maids of Elfin-Mere," which had appeared first in *Poems* under the title "The Maidens of the Mere." Allingham added a chorus to the new version which effectively reinforces the mood of far-off unhappy romance. *"Years ago, and years ago, And the tall reeds sigh as the wind doth blow."* The poem was illustrated by a characteristic woodcut from the hand of D.G. Rossitti, depicting the three rapt spinning maidens and the love-lorn Pastor's son at their feet.

In addition to ballads proper Allingham wrote many songs. These range from the ballad type (it would be difficult to distinguish between song and ballad in "Nanny's Sailor Lad") to the children's songs, which were probably the most popular of Allingham's writings with his Victorian readers. Many of these seem insipid, even for Victorian childish taste, and would hardly appeal to children today. For example, "The Bird" begins:

Birdie, Birdie, will you pet?
Summertime is far away yet
You'll have silken quilts and a velvet bed
And a pillow of satin for your head!

"Robin Redbreast", a much better poem, though it does rather sentimentalize the robin, was very popular indeed with Victorian readers; but the most justly famous of his children's songs is "The Fairies":

Up the airy mountain
    Down the rushy glen,
We daren't go a-hunting
    For fear of little men,
Wee folk, good folk,
    Trooping all together;
Green jacket, red cap,
    And white owl's feather.

George Saintsbury, in the *Cambridge History of English Literature* after misquoting the title (Up the Fairy Mountain) dismissed this poem by saying that it "borrows its first and best stanza from one of the most beautiful Jacobite ballads and entirely fails to live up to it."

Patrick MacDonogh reports being unable to trace this ballad after considerable research in the ballad books. It seems more likely that Allingham took a hint, not from the ballad Saintsbury refers to, ("Up the craggy mountain,/ And down the mossy glen/ He daurna go a-milking/ For Charlie and his men.") but from a child's singing-game known as "Round About the Punch Bowl". It goes as follows:

Round about the punch bowl, once, twice, three,
The last time they catch him they'll not catch me,
Lizzie made a pudding so nice and so sweet,
Saying - haste love, haste love, don't say nay,
For next Sunday morning to church we will go.
Rings on her fingers and bells on her toes
With her baby on her knee, and through the world
                                        she goes,
Up the heathery mountain and down the rushy glen
We daren't go a-hunting for Corner and his men.

"Corner" originally referred to a Fairy Chief, but in Jacobite times it was used for Prince Charlie. It seems probable that there is an oral tradition behind both song and ballad, stretching back into the mists of time. Allingham says nothing about the origin of his song; he merely records in his diary that he wrote it at Killybegs in January, 1849, whither he had gone on customs duty.

Clearly he was not trying to reconstruct a Jacobite ballad but to write a fairy song, and if his opening lines are traditional he uses them successfully for his own purpose. The song is trivial enough but it has a delicate and easy grace of movement, a singing charm.

Allingham was not limited to children's songs, of course. Many of his best short poems have the movement of song. He makes good use of chorus in "The Ruined Chapel", where the monotonous and persistent flow of time is suggested by the repeated fourth line in every verse: "And Day and Night and Day go by" and in "The Mowers", a simple but attractive pastoral song, that goes to the rhythm of the scythe. "A scythe-sweep, and a scythe-sweep,/ We mow the grass together."

We have seen that Allingham's roots are in Ballyshannon and that his poetry begins with the sounds and sights of his boyhood. But his relationship with Ballyshannon was by no means just a simple love and admiration. Like every other Irish poet he was deeply engaged in a conflict of love and hate with his home environment. Although love predominates there are times when he cries out against "this desolate Ballyshannon village." For all his nostalgic descriptions in his autobiographical fragment and in some of his poems, such as "The Winding Banks of Erne", he was well aware of the seamier sides of life in the back streets of Ballyshannon. In a contribution he made to *The Ballyshannon Almanac*

(1862) he points out "dilapidated houses, rows of hovels shutting up the river bank," the poverty behind the picturesque facade.

Yet it was not rural poverty and neglect that chiefly depressed Allingham but the complete lack of educated society. His literary pursuits elicited little sympathy from his family and relatives, and his isolation was made worse by his nonconformity in religious and other matters. He confessed his wretchedness in a letter to Henry Sutton written in June, 1849:

> I am in ill-health, and in wrong relations with nearly everyone around me from non-conformity on my part and non-sympathy on theirs. . .intercourse with my relatives is a constant pain and disgust (unremovable in the nature of things and yet shocking one as a sin) and I read *The Dial* like one in a strange country.

A few years later, in February, 1852, he had a brief note from Coventry Patmore in London urging him to form a Rifle Club in Ballyshannon. (In England there had been a great scare about the possibility of an invasion by Louis Napoleon.) Patmore must have been sadly ignorant of the condition of Ireland ever to make such a suggestion. Allingham trenchantly disabuses him, pointing out that the most militant spirits in Ireland are already either Ribbonmen or Orangemen, and that *The Nation* newspaper "frequently touches on the advantages and opportunities to be hoped from a foreign invasion of England." His letter ends with a cry of loneliness:

> I wish I could make you think it a *duty* to exchange a few written words with me now and again. It is like visiting a man in prison. Consider and have charity (in the intervals of

rifle practice) on the condition of a gregarious, conversational person in a desolate island. I know everybody here, and so know thoroughly that there is nobody. I don't speak in contempt, believe, and I always *think* kindly of people, —but I mention, thus, the sure and well-tried state of things.

And it is not alone, or chiefly, the want of high intellectual intercourse that distresses me, but that one and all of the finer ingredients of social life are absent, —to a curious and almost incredible degree.

Some five years later in June, 1857, we find him writing to Mrs. Howitt with similar complaints about lack of conversation and companionship, and the unsympathetic nature of those closest to him. The letter reveals very clearly both the satisfactions and the frustrations of his life in Ireland:

Life here is monotonous as ever—no conversations—no new acquaintances. Commanding points attained in walking or reading are the landmarks. . .This is dated at Ballyshannon, but written at Burdoran, 4 miles off, in a pleasant room looking over the blue sea sparkling with little waves. I bathed this morning in a deep rockbound creek—brown sealeaves waving below in the pure green depth. Now, if you are in London and this comes to you on a hot dusty day, you'll begin to envy me, but let me tell you that I have, in the act of writing this letter, spilt the inkbottle over a new tablecloth and that *there is somebody in the room who doesn't yet know of this, and who will be excessively angry.* (in a footnote he adds: 'You as a housekeeper will sympathise with the accuser; but *it wasn't my fault*—the table came in two!) How pleasant many places would be, if pleasant people lived there.

Three years after this, in June 1860, he wrote to Mrs. Browning from London. At the end of his letter he says: "I go back to silent little Ballyshannon (save for the constant moan of the waterfall) next week. Do send me a letter during the summer—you cannot conceive the gift it is." Ballyshannon was a pleasant, indeed a beautiful place—for walking, swimming, sometimes skating—(a pastime he deeply enjoyed), and for reading; but for conversation and companionship he had nowhere to turn.

3

Laurence Bloomfield
in Ireland

Laurence Bloomfield is much the most important poem that Allingham wrote, and it springs directly out of his awareness of the Ireland that he knew, and his own special viewpoint, which was neither Orange nor Green. Before examining the poem, it is worthwhile considering his approach to religion and politics.

He once noted in his diary, after he had spent an evening in Lymington playing old Irish airs on his violin: "I love Ireland: were she only not Catholic! but would she be Ireland otherwise?" It is interesting to speculate what difference it would have made to Allingham's life and writing if he had been born into a Catholic family. Would he have felt more at one with the people of Ireland? Would he have espoused the Nationalist cause? Of course, quite a number of young men born into Protestant families in the nineteenth century became Nationalists. There is John Mitchell, for example, but Mitchel had a temperament utterly different from Allingham's. Both by temper and by upbringing Allingham leaned away from partisanship and involvement in Irish politics. In Geoffrey Taylor's words he was "that impossible thing, an Irish liberal."

His childhood was not free from the shadow of fear caused by "rebel" demonstrations and he naturally absorbed the sympathies of the class he belonged to; yet he was able in later life to be friendly with the Roman Catholic Bishop, Dr. McGettigan. His own words in his fragment of autobiography reveal vividly the problems of growing up in nineteenth-century Ireland:

> I came early to the consciousness that I was living in a discontented and disloyal country; it seemed the natural state of things that the humbler class—which was almost synonymous with Roman Catholic, should hate those above them in the world, and lie in wait for a chance of despoiling them. Yet I never for a moment believed this of any of the *individuals* of this class amongst whom I lived. I used to fancy and sometimes dream frightfully of a swarm of fierce men seizing the town, bursting into the houses, etc., of soldiers drawn out in rank with levelled guns, of firing, bloodshed, and all horror.

> Once there was something like an approach to realisation. It must have been at a time when our garrison was temporarily withdrawn or reduced to a detachment, that a rude army of 'Whiteboys' actually marched through the town, armed with scythes, pikes, and I know not what. I was turned six years old then. I remember being at the corner of our lane, holding somebody's hand or lifted in somebody's arms, and have a most dim yet authentic memory-picture of a dark wild procession of men, crowded closely together, holding and brandishing things over their heads. It streamed past us up the long hill of the Main Street, and I daresay I was taken home before it had passed by, for in the dim picture it is always seen passing on and up interminably, a

dark throng with pikes and scythes held aloft. I looked with curiosity unmixed with dread; but it was probably after this that the dread showed itself in dramatic forms in my dreams.

In spite of these dark memories Allingham described Ballyshannon as a "sort of island of peace" and he could not recall any actual offence by a political or secret society within the town or district. The local Parish Priest, Father John Cummins, was a peace-loving and peace-making man, who was on very good neighborly terms with Allingham's father.

Later in his life Allingham was on friendly terms with Daniel McGettigan, who became Bishop of the Catholic diocese of Raphoe (Co.Donegal) and lived in Ballyshannon. Allingham, who disliked most prelates of whatever church, admired and respected the Bishop for his frugal, blameless life, his dignity and devotion to his calling— "more like by far to one's notion of a 'primitive Bishop' than any other prelate I have seen." Recording in his diary a chance meeting with McGettigan in a Dublin hotel in 1865, he describes him as "a tall, very comely man, with a pleasant brogue and simple manners" and then exclaims, "if he were only not a Bishop!"

As we would expect from his upbringing and attitudes Allingham approaches the troubled Irish scene from the viewpoint of an honest and sympathetic observer. The opening statement of his Preface to the first complete edition (1864) is a fair account of his aim:

In this poem on every-day Irish affairs (a new and difficult, and for more than one reason a ticklish literary experiment), all readers who know Ireland will certainly see a good deal of truth, not taken up at second-hand. . .it is free from personalities, and neither of an orange nor a green complexion; but it is Irish in phraseology, character, and local colour, —with as little use as might be of a corrupt dialect, and with no deference at all to the stage traditions of Paddyism.

Allingham had begun work on *Bloomfield* in Ballyshannon, and continued it after his move to Lymington. In correspondence with Rossetti he refers to it as 'the Sawdust Poem', and expresses fears that the subject is too earthy and unromantic. In March 1860 he wrote:

I am doing something occasionally at a poem on Irish matters, to have two thousand lines or so, and can see my way through it. One part out of three is done. But alas! when all's done, who will like it? Think of the Landlord and Tenant Question in flat decasyllables! Did you ever hear of the Irish coaster that was hailed, 'Smack ahoy! What's your cargo?' 'Timber and fruit!' 'What sort?' 'Besoms and potatoes!' I fear my poem will no better fulfil expectations.

Three years later when the poem was finished (it was nearer 5,000 than 2,000 lines) he confided a little rhyme about it to his diary:

A story in 5000 lines,
Where Homer's epic fervour shines,
    Philosophy like Plato's—
Alas, I sing of Paddies, Priests,
And Pigs, those unromantic beasts,
    Policemen and Potatoes!

Allingham need not have worried on the score of his subject matter; the poem has weaknesses but it is full of interest just because it does deal with the mundane and sordid detail of Irish rural life.

The poem first appeared in *Fraser's* magazine, in twelve monthly installments running from November 1862 to November 1863 (one month was missed). Allingham had evidently completed the first four chapters before the serial publication started, but the remaining eight he wrote month by month, under some pressure at times. In his diary he complained "It's not properly compacted as to plan," and he revised the poem for publication in book form but it still has basically the same twelve chapters and the sequence of the story is not altered.

Since the poem has been out of print for many years and copies of it are extremely rare I give first an outline of the narrative. The central figure, we might call him hero, is Laurence Bloomfield, a young Irish landlord, heir to Croghan Hall and the estates belonging to it. Nursed fondly by "a Celtic peasant", he had left Ireland for an English school at the age of twelve. At school, encouraged by an Irish friend, he became an ardent Irish patriot, but as a student at Cambridge his views changed. Impressed by the "large imperial tone," the might of England's monarchy and the majesty of her laws, he swings to an Orange viewpoint. But his British enthusiasm fades, too, and at the age of twenty-six, after much travel and reading he returns to Ireland, with an open, independent mind.

At this point the story proper begins, with Laurence riding meditatively to a dinner party at the house of his Uncle, Sir Ulick Harvey, a haughty squire, owner of Lisnamoy House and large estates. Laurence observes the contrast between the hovels of the peasants and his uncle's lordly mansion. The neighboring landlords are described in unflattering terms: Lord Crashton, elderly profligate absentee; Finlay, a hard but honest man; Dysart, shiftless descendant of an ancient family, encumbered with debt in a decaying house; Isaac Brown, shrewd, money-making Wesleyan; *the* O'Hara, a rigid Catholic, worn with care.

The guests at dinner include several of these landlords and some local politicians. All are concerned with the state of the country, where landlords and tenants are living as foes. Their county (almost certainly based on Co.Donegal) is notorious for agrarian crime. The Orange view—"All papists are but rebels in disguise"—is loudly proclaimed by "great Nassau Blunderbore"; and Pigot, land agent both to Sir Ulick and to Laurence on their neighbouring estates, argues for the removal of the peasants living in a mountain tract to which they have no legal right. Their hamlet, Ballytullagh, is a nest of Ribbonmen.

Laurence rides home early from the dinner party profoundly disturbed in mind and spirit. He is tempted to withdraw from Ireland and her troubles, but he recognizes his duty and resolves to face the challenge.

The scene changes to the humble cottage of the Dorans. Jack Doran's father, desperately poor, had struggled to cultivate a waste corner between harsh mountain and black bogland. Now Jack and Maureen, his wife, still poor but hardworking and prospering, have improved their little corner, but have no legal title to it. They are at the mercy of Pigot, the agent, who has noted their improvements. The family—a bright son, Neal, and an attractive daughter, Bridget—have thought of going to America, but Maureen is old for change and Jack is attached to his bit of land. Neal, conscious of the injustice of landlord rule in Ireland, is drawn toward Ballytullagh and the Ribbon Lodge.

Pigot is at war with Ballytullagh and intends to evict those whose rent is in arrears. Some evictions have already taken place and the Ribbon-men retaliate with a

threat to Pigot's life, signed by "Captain Starlight".
Father John Adair warns the people against Ribbonism,
but his words have little effect. Neal finally takes the
oath and joins the Ribbon Lodge, together with Denis,
his sister's sweetheart. Under a strong escort of armed
police the evictions at Ballytullagh are carried out, the
hearth fires extinguished, roofs and walls battered
down. A raffle, followed by a dance, is held to assist one
of the evicted, a girl dying of consumption.

There is a meeting of the local Ribbon Lodge in a
back-street at Lisnamoy, at which the decision is taken
to give Jeremy Burke a "dry-beating" because he had
offered to negotiate for a farm from which a neighbor
had been turned out. At the end of the meeting those in
the inner ring are told that approval has come for the
death sentence on Pigot. There is a fair at Lisnamoy and
Neal and Denis are given the task of revealing Jeremy
Burke to two strangers who will deal with him. But they
get involved in a brawl with the tinkers in the fair, are
arrested and brought before the local magistrate. Since
Neal is Pigot's man, he is sent for. Pigot, attending the
fair with Laurence, to receive rents and give orders for
more evictions, has been given by an informer a complete list of those in the local Ribbon Lodge, which he
hands to Bloomfield, while he goes to the court intend-
ing to get Neal and Denis detained because their names
are on the list.

Laurence is left alone, unhappy about the pending
evictions, knowing that he must take the reins of power
from Pigot, but uncertain when and how to do it. The
sight of the timid tenant throng waiting patiently, especially "Jack Doran with his toilworn face," works on

him. When Jack falls in a faint at the news that his son has been arrested on Ribbon business, Laurence decides to act at once. He dismisses Pigot, burns the Ribbon list and offers a new deal to his tenants, in which landlord and tenant will cooperate to improve the land and the holders' security. Neal and Denis are set free.

Meanwhile the dismissed Pigot is driving home in his gig to Newbridge House, where his wife anxiously awaits him. He is ambushed and shot dead.

The narrative thread of the poem really ends at this point in chapter ten. The last two chapters are retrospective and inform us of the changes that have taken place during the seven years of Laurence's rule over his estates. He is now married to Jane, a perfect wife, who shares his ideals of uplifting the peasantry, and they have two delightful children, Mary and Fred. The countryside and the town are vastly improved. "The smoky hovel with its fetid pool" has disappeared; everywhere there are snug cottages, trim gates and fences, and the land has been improved by drainage and afforestation. In the town there is a new marketplace and town hall, a cozy inn, "The Bloomfield Arms" and a model secular school; even the workhouse has been reformed.

The final chapter shows us Laurence and Jane entertaining their friends at Croghan Hall, boating on the lough, discussing Irish politics and land problems. We are given news of various characters in the earlier story. Finally, Laurence and Jane, the night before they leave for a holiday in Norway, climb a local mountain and look down over Ireland, thinking of its beauty and its sorrows.

There is clearly a large element of day-dream in the

last two books, but despite this the story is an absorbing and moving one; it might easily have been written as a novel. As it is, the couplets run easily and freely in the main, and though it has faults of design and arrangement it seems to me wrong to call it "dull", as Yeats and others did.

Perhaps the first thing that strikes a reader of Allingham is the new force that seems to enter his descriptive writing when he depicts the state of the countryside. Almost at the outset we have a piece of somber landscape-painting reminiscent of Crabbe:

> The cornstacks seen through rusty sycamores,
> Pigs, tatter'd children, pools at cabin doors,
> Unshelter'd rocky hillsides, browsed by sheep,
> Summer's last flow'rs that nigh some brooklet creep
> Black flats of bog, stone-fences loose and rough,
> A thorn-branch in a gap thought gate enough,
> And all the wide and groveless landscape round,
> Moor, stubble, aftermath, or new plough'd ground,
> Where with the crows, white seagulls come to pick;
> Or many a wasteful acre crowded thick
> With docken, coltsfoot, and the hoary weed
> Call'd fairy-horse, and tufted thistle-seed
> Which *for* the farm, *against* the farmer tells;
> Or wrinkled hawthorns shading homestead wells,
> Or saddest sight, some ruin'd cottage-wall,
> The roof-tree cut, the rafters forced to fall. . .

Allingham is here writing with an observant eye focused on a clearly recognizable Irish landscape; this is something we miss in many of his lyrical poems, where the natural background is often vague and unrealized, lacking specific detail. In the lyrical poems we rarely get a dismal scene, though there are descriptions of storm and tempest. In *Laurence Bloomfield* the summer

glories of lough and mountain are balanced by scenes of
wintry desolation:

> But now, all round, with dark and doleful hues
> A sombre sky the sluggish bog imbues;
> Black pit and pool, coarse tuft and quaking marsh,
> Stretch far away to mountains chill and harsh
> Under the lowering clouds; while, near at hand,
> The waters grey in trench and furrow stand.

Not only the Irish landscape but the interiors of
houses and cabins are painted with harsh truth without
any of the ideal softening that we find in *The Music
Master* and other poems. Here is the hovel in Ballytullagh where Rose Muldoon lies ill:

> Bare grimy walls, a roof with many a flaw,
> This corner strewn with turf, and that with straw,
> A borrow'd bedstead, two old stools, no more,
> To furnish round the damp uneven floor,
> Three plates, three broken cups, an iron pot,
> A batter'd black tin-porringer kept hot
> Beside the gaping hearth, enough to choke
> The unaccustom'd lungs with lazy smoke,—
> Such was the house:

The account of the fair at Lisnamoy in chapter nine,
is particularly good. It is not simply a sordid scene; it
has its cheerful and amusing sides, and a great deal of
bustling, noisy life. There is something of the crowded
vitality of a peasant scene by Breughel in Allingham's
picture of pedlars, tinkers, gamblers, old-clothesmen,
apple-sellers, beggars, and so on. One passage describes
the 'jobbers'—dealers in cattle or horses—striking a bargain by spitting on a coin and clapping it into the seller's
hand.

> Mud hovels fringe the 'Fair-green' of this town
> A spot misnamed, at every season brown,
> O'erspread with countless man and beast to-day,

Which bellow, squeak, and shout, bleat, bray and neigh.
The 'jobbers' there, each more or less a rogue,
Noisy, or smooth, with each his various brogue.
Cool wiry Dublin, Connaught's golden mouth,
Blunt Northern, plaintive sing-song of the South,
Feel cattle's ribs, or jaws of horses try
For truth, since men's are very sure to lie,
And shun with parrying blow and practised heed
The rushing horns, the wildly prancing steed.
The moisten'd penny greets with sounding smack
The rugged palm, which smites the greeting back;
Oaths fly, the bargain like a quarrel burns,
And oft the buyer turns, and oft returns;
Now mingle Sassanach and Gaelic tongue;
On either side are slow concessions wrung;
An anxious audience interfere, at last
The sale is closed, and whiskey binds it fast
In cave of quilting upon oziers bent,
With many an ancient patch and breezy rent.

It would not be unfair to say that Allingham's lyrical
poetry reveals mostly feminine qualities of musical
sweetness, grace, and charm. *Laurence Bloomfield* reveals unexpected masculine qualities in his verse. Not
only are there powerful realistic scenes, like the fair at
Lisnamoy, or the eviction scene in chapter seven, but
the character sketches of local people have a keen ironic
edge. Nothing in Allingham's earlier poetry prepares us
for this, though it flashes out again in his later aphorisms and epigrams. One can't help noticing how much
better are the satiric portraits of the landlords than the
idealized portrait of "Queen Jane", Bloomfield's perfect
wife, in chapter eleven. Allingham uses the couplet
form, lending itself to neat balance, antithesis, and epigram, with considerable skill in these portraits. He had
clearly learned a good deal from Pope and Crabbe. Lord
Crashton, the absentee landlord, is dismissed as follows:

My Lord, with gouty legs,
Drinks Baden-Baden water, and life's dregs,
With cynic jest inlays his black despair,
And curses all things from his easy chair.

One of his best portraits is that of Isaac Brown, a shrewd and wealthy Wesleyan who "takes a quiet bill at ten per cent." When the spirit moves him he is given to long outbursts of extempore prayer in the local chapel:

Handorgan-wise the holy phrases ground,
Go turning and returning round and round;
The sing-song duly runs from low to high;
The choruss'd groans at intervals reply;
Till after forty minutes' sweat and din,
Leaving perhaps too little prayer within,
Dear Brother Brown, athletic babe of grace,
Resumes his bench, and wipes his reeking face.

Allingham is good at catching the tone and reasoning of those whose political views he does not share. Here, for example is Dr. Larmour, "An Antrim Presbyterian, short and spare," roundly dismissing Irish nationalism:

Ireland, forsooth, 'a nation once again!'
If Ireland was a nation, tell me when?
For since the civil modern world began
What's Irish History? Walks the child a man?
Or strays he still perverse and immature,
Weak, slothful, rash, irresolute, unsure;
Right bonds rejecting, hugging rusty chains,
Nor one clear view; nor one bold step attains?
What Ireland might have been if wisely school'd,
I know not: far too briefly Cromwell ruled.
We see the melting of a barbarous race,
Sad sight, I grant, sir, from their ancient place;
But always, everywhere, it has been so;
Red-Indians, Bushmen, Irish—they must go!"

The chief weakness of the poem lies in its arrangement; it is sprawling and discursive. A judicious use of the blue pencil would much improve it, and it could be considerably reduced in length. In chapter six the narrative is cut to a slender thread, and we are given a long summary of ancient Irish history. In chapter ten, where the whole story gathers to a crisis and the narrative is moving rapidly, we are held up, just when we want to learn the fate of Pigot, by a lengthy description of Mrs. Pigot and her home, that would have been much more acceptable in the opening stages of the story. At the beginning of chapters ten and eleven there are quite unneccessary apologetic addresses to the reader, which only reveal Allingham's lack of self-confidence. "Alas you count me a prosaic bard/ Good reader! Think what Horace says, how hard/ It is to sing of every-day affairs. . ." He apologizes to Maiden and Boy for not offering more romantic entertainment: "Ye cannot love such dismal verse as mine." We know from Allingham's letters that he really thought highly of *Laurence Bloomfield*, but from these remarks he appears unaware that he is writing a much finer poem than *The Music Master* and that one of its greatest virtues is its firm anchorage in the prosaic reality of Irish life. In fact the weakest parts of the poem are precisely those where he departs furthest from prosaic reality, as in the idealised ending, and the rather crude and melodramatic account of the Ribbon Lodge.

Working throughout the poem and giving it an underlying strength are two strong and sincere emotions; one is a deep compassion for the hard life of the Irish peasant, the other a deep love of Ireland. Allingham does not gloss over the squalor and shiftlessness of the peasants of Ballytullagh, but he defends them from the usual criticisms of the landlord class. These people cannot change their way of life; they are so near the bottom that they have no room to maneuver:

> When all goes well, are one degree, no more
> From want; grim Hunger, always at the door,
> With scarce a push comes in when aught goes wrong.
> —Why hold their land? Why marry? Why this throng
> Of naked children? Would you heap the rates
> By help beyond the loathsome Poorhouse gates?
> Why not take other work? —I tell you why:
> There is no work: they needs must beg, or fly,
> (O happy chance!) or else lie down and die.

Allingham's deep sympathy with "toilful Irish hands" (in a letter to Ferguson he exclaimed: "Politics or no Politics, I would give the waste lands of Ireland into toilful Irish hands") comes out most fully in his treatment of Jack Doran, who has worked hard all his life, cautiously kept clear of all Ribbon activities, but finds himself at the mercy of an agent's whim. Pigot gives him three weeks to leave "that poor spot of earth" where sixty years ago he was born. He waits in the queue with others, equally humble and timid, for a chance to plead his case with the agent. Allingham had known men like Jack Doran; in his diary he refers to meeting "Jack McNulty (who *partly* sat for Jack Doran)." The deep compassion for the laboring poor that flickers in Gray's *Elegy* and smolders darkly in Crabbe's *The Village*, burns steadily through Allingham's couplets.

> The wife, the babes, that Heavenly Bounty gave
> Increase his load of fetters on the slave;
> His sweat absorb'd into a patch of earth,
> His life-long labours held of little worth,
> Dependent hourly on a rich man's whim,
> Whose busy idleness regards not him.

No foot of ground, however wild, he owns,
Till in the graveyard rest his weary bones,

Both Laurence Bloomfield and his creator stood aloof from large political schemes for Ireland, but they both firmly believed that peasant ownership should be encouraged, that waste lands, and lands falling vacant on indebted estates, should be given to those who would cultivate them. Laurence, who resembles Allingham in many respects, is clearly expressing his creator's love of Ireland in his final meditation on the land that lies below him. He is saddened by the thought of all those who are forced to leave Ireland, like his own nurse, whose Gaelic song about Holy Ireland's plenteous cheer he still recalls. At the end it is his wife who encourages him to continue in hope:

"This mild green country in the western sea
With guardian mountains, rivers full and free,
Home of a brave, rich-brained, warm-hearted race,—
This Ireland should have been a noble place."

"It will be," Jane replied.

4

Later Poetry: Stories, Moral Essays, and Epigrams

In the last years of his life Allingham began to make a collection of his verse in six volumes. (See Bibliography.) Most of his best work, which I have already discussed, is to be found in the first and fourth of these volumes, *Irish Songs and Poems* and *Laurence Bloomfield,* though there is a scattering of good lyrics in the other volumes. Allingham was ill-advised to make a six-volume collection; all his weakest work is carefully preserved and his best work is dispersed. His reputation would have been better served by a judicious selection; but he was too close to his own work and too susceptible to many of the weaker aspects of Victorian taste to be a good self-critic. There seems to have been little demand for this collected edition. Indeed, Allingham hardly expected the public to respond to his work, he had been so often disappointed in the past. His dedication to *Thought and Word* is apologetic, even rather pathetic:

TO MY CHILDREN
hoping they (if no others) will bring
a sympathetic attention to these endeavours
to put in words
some faint hint of the highest truths—
inexpressible in any form of language.

After *Laurence Bloomfield* his new work mostly
appeared in *Fifty Modern Poems* (1865), *Evil May Day*
(1882), and *Blackberries* (1884). It can be roughly
divided into stories in verse, moral exhortations, and
epigrams or short pieces.

The best of the stories in verse is "George Levison, or
The Schoolfellows". Allingham sent it to Dickens for
Household Words in 1857 and Dickens replied: "I am
happy to retain the Poem, which is mournfully true, and
has moved me very much." George Levison (Allingham
changed the name to Hildebrand in a later version) is an
old school friend of the teller of the story. The latter
lives with Annie, his beloved wife, and their small son in
a quiet village. One summer evening, George calls at
their door and it soon becomes apparent that the
splendid promise of his school days has come to
nothing; he is a penniless drunkard who begs a spare
coat. He leaves the village next morning as abruptly as
he came and later comes news of his death. "Through all
the summer-time/ The touch of that unhappy visit lay/
Like trace of frost on gardens, on our life." It is a pity
that Allingham did not end with these words. He goes
on to meditate and to moralize for another twenty-five
lines. The poem does succeed in suggesting the painful
contrast between the blissful couple and the ruined
man, who has squandered his talents and his soul; and
their embarrassed inability to give any effective help.

But the poem comes perilously near to sentimentality and cliché. Almost half of it is devoted to painting a picture of domestic bliss, and one can't help feeling that Allingham is indulging himself in a daydream of the life he longed for. At the same time he does succeed in conveying the peaceful uneventful life of the village whose chief excitement was the arrival of the post in the evenings. The village is clearly Ballyshannon, even to the Allingham's rose bush, here "the great Whiterose-bush" which "lean'd A thousand tender little heads" from the garden wall.

"Southwell Park", which first appeared in *Fifty Modern Poems*, is a melodramatic story telling how a young bridegroom's bower of bliss at Southwell Park is destroyed by the sudden appearance of a woman he has seduced. The desperate woman drowns herself in sight of the bride and groom, and the beautiful park remains closed and empty. There is some skillful descriptive writing but the characters remain shadowy and unreal.

The same is true of "Mervaunee", which is set in ancient Ireland. (In a later version the title becomes "The Lady of the Sea: A Legend of Ancient Erin.") Prince Dalimar marries a woman of the sea but she pines for her home and finally returns to it. One moonlit night the prince dives into the sea from his ship to rejoin her. The poem moves between natural and supernatural, and never really comes alive. In both poems the kernel of narrative is slight and small, almost as though it were providing an excuse for descriptive writing. "A Stormy Night," subtitled "A Story of the Donegal Coast," comes closer to the life Allingham knew, and it has a pleasing little prologue depicting Ballyshannon. An ex-

hausted survivor from a shipwreck is apparently murdered, for his money, by his own brother, but the man
survives, and the wicked brother, crazed with guilt, and
thinking he has seen a ghost, disappears forever. The tale
is highly melodramatic, but it moves with some speed
and excitement.

"Evil May Day" has little to recommend it. Allingham was all his life a strong Deist, although his God
belonged to no church or chapel, and he shared fully the
intense moral earnestness that characterized most thinking Victorians. As he grew older he seemed to find it
necessary to affirm continually his belief in the ultimate
significance of the universe, in God and Goodness. Part I
of "May-Day" expresses his horror at awakening one
May morning to the conviction that there is no God; but
in Parts II and III he recovers his faith. The poem has
neither the intellectual substance nor the personal passion to make it interesting. Its moral earnestness remains
flat; and so does the blank verse:

> May-Day was evil when I miss'd my God;
> Earth, sea and sky fall'n empty of a sudden.
> All the wide universe a dismal waste
> Peopled with phantoms of my flitting self,
> And mocking gleams chance-kindled and chance-quench'd,
> All meaning nothing.

When Allingham writes poetry of moral exhortation
he moves furthest from his real poetic roots, his power
of observing places and people and his own feelings. The
more abstract he becomes the thinner and flatter his
poetry. In "News from Pannonia" he attempts a dia-
logue between two Roman citizens reporting the death
of Marcus Aurelius and extolling his philosophy of life.
He states the great truths, the great moral common-

places, that Aurelius expressed, with some skill but the poem never comes alive. It remains a kind of literary and historical exercise.

The same might be said of a Victorian-Shakespearian play that Allingham wrote entitled *Ashby Manor.* The time is June, 1645, after the battle of Naseby, when a defeated Royalist Cavalry Officer seeks refuge at the home of the Colonel of Horse on the Parliamentary side. It is a story of gallantry and romance, ending in the union of the two lovers on opposite sides in the Civil War, and the defeat of a scheming rival. The play, in mixed verse and prose, has faded Shakespearian echoes. It is entirely English in every way. There is even a Devonshire countryman, Tom Trivet, servant to the Cavalry Officer, who speaks a broad Devonshire dialect.

The best of Allingham's later verse is to be found in *Blackberries,* first published in 1884 and later reprinted as the last of the six collected volumes. He had a certain flair for the epigram and the short satiric verse, though he is diffident and apologetic about this book too. He wrote to Samuel Ferguson: "I have a little book in the press called "Blackberries', aphoristic and epigrammatic, which will please nobody and yet out it must come." When it appeared he sent a copy to his friend F. G. Stephens, who was art critic for the *Athenaeum,* describing it as "a queerish little basket of 'Blackberries'. . .many being indigestible. . ." The book is prefaced by the following epigram:

"Who buys Blackberries?—Asking, sir, your pardon
Can't you bring us something that will sell at Covent Garden?
Flourish Covent Garden and Paternoster Row;
But let the birds and gypsies their own ways go."

The dedication is "For Anybody", and there is a general air of take-it-or-leave-it about the tone in which Allingham presents his basket of "Blackberries". At the end of the book he puts this tailpiece: "If a single verse you find/ Palatable to your mind,/ Be that the core, the rest the rind." If the book is approached in this spirit the reader will find many berries that have a palatable juice in them, though it is a book to be browsed in rather than read through. The aphorisms and epigrams are arranged according to theme—Religion, Love, Politics, Literature, etc. Too many items are packed into Allingham's basket; he always seemed reluctant to abandon anything he had written. He is often at his best when briefest; many of the two-line epigrams make their point effectively:

> Not men and women in an Irish street
> But Catholics and Protestants you meet.

Perhaps readers should be reminded that this was written in the Victorian period. How much have Irish streets changed in the last hundred years?

> Who speaks to a crowd
> Should be plain, brief and loud.

This simple advice is still worth remembering, even if public-address systems have made the last word inapplicable.

> England! leave Asia, Africa, alone.
> And mind this little country of thine own.

English men and women might have been happier had this advice been followed. *Blackberries* reminds us of Allingham's radicalism; he was opposed to Britain's imperialist wars in Afghanistan and Zululand. There is a sonnet "In Snow" enlisting sympathy for an Afghan youth, "Shot by the stranger on his native hills," and another, "Words and Deeds", protesting against English talk of Justice and Brotherhood, while their deadly weapons mowed down the ranks of Zulu warriors.

Here are a few more sample "blackberries", without comment:

INSCRIPTION OMITTED ON A PUBLIC MONUMENT
Look, and receive admonishment from me:
Such as I was, take good care not to be.

PLUS ULTRA
"Count no man happy ere his death'. And then
May come the foolish biographic pen.

———————————

Is idleness indeed so black a crime?
What are the Busy doing, half their time?

ADVICE TO A YOUNG POET
You're a true poet: but, my dear,
If you would hold the public ear,
Remember to be *not too clear*
Be strange, be verbally intense;
Words matter ten times more than sense. . .

In this volume, as occasionally elsewhere, Allingham reveals a somewhat unexpected vein of gentle astringency, which reminds us of his friend, Arthur Hugh Clough. This vein is most in evidence perhaps when he deals with politics and public affairs. He wrote a neat little epigram "To a Primrose", when that modest flower was adopted as an emblem by Disraeli and the Tory party. Certainly his small wild "blackberries" are far more acceptable than his long-winded moral exhortations in verse.

5

Prose Writings

All his life Allingham was, in his own phrase, a
"Poetry-Worshipper", but on many occasions he expressed the desire or the intention of writing in prose. In
a letter to his friend Henry Sutton, dated 18 October,
1850, he says:

> I want to write a little prose book speaking plainly and
> quite uncompromisingly of several matters, —but don't
> know how to set about it. I wish to introduce bits of
> characters, humour, scenery, criticism and so on; I have
> in turn chosen and rejected the forms of Tale, Letters,
> Diary, Dialogue and all these mixed. Many a time I have
> hit upon what seemed *the* plan while going to bed,
> turned it over and over until it expanded into the mist
> of dreams, and found it vanish almost as rapidly in the
> next day's light.

He never did quite find a wholly satisfactory prose
form, though he wrote a great deal of prose in the
course of his writing life. It is perhaps a pity that he
never tried a novel, though it is doubtful if he could
have handled an extended story successfully. He had
many of the qualities needed in a novelist; a keen obser-

vation of people and things, an eye and an ear for detail, and a sense of the mystery and uniqueness of every human being.

His most important prose work is undoubtedly his diary. Possibly he intended to use it simply as the basis of the autobiography that he had no more than begun at the time of his death. The fragment he left is excellent and he might have written a fine autobiography. But it is equally possible that the account of his adult life would not have maintained the freshness and charm of his opening chapter. The diary we have, edited by his widow and a friend, remains in its original diary form, unrevised and unexpanded by the writer. Mrs. Allingham omitted some portions of it, and these have unfortunately since been destroyed. Francis Bickley was able to consult them when he was writing *The Pre-Raphaelite Comedy* (1932), and to judge from a few brief passages that he quotes, Mrs. Allingham omitted things that might have given offense by a certain asperity, and also those things that might have thrown an unfavorable light on her husband. The diary is not intensely personal or confessional, though it does reveal the man who wrote it, as well as providing many detailed accounts of famous Victorian men and women. Allingham, like Boswell, had an eye for those trivial and mundane details, that do so much to bring back to life a past age. He notices and records the smoking habits of Carlyle and Tennyson; the physical shape of Spurgeon the preacher ("big body, short legs, flat feet"), the face and voice and dress of Ouida. He had also a retentive ear for conversation, and records what passed at the breakfast table, the dinner table, and in the street.

Allingham worshipped Tennyson all his life as a Great Poet and a Great Man (though he was not uncritical and did not share the general admiration for "Maud") and Tennyson gets expansive treatment in the diary. One of the great moments of the young Irishman's life was his first meeting with Tennyson at Twickenham; the meeting was arranged by Coventry Patmore and took place on 28 June, 1851:

> I was admitted, shown upstairs into a room with books lying about, and soon came in a tall, broad-shouldered swarthy man, slightly stooping, with loose dark hair and beard. He wore spectacles and was obviously very near-sighted. Hollow cheeks and the dark pallor of his skin gave him an unhealthy appearance. He was a strange and almost spectral figure. The Great Man peered close at me, and then shook hands cordially, yet with a profound quietude of manner. He was then about forty-one, but looked much older, from his bulk, his short-sight, stooping shoulders, and loose careless dress.

Allingham was invited to stay for dinner, "which I was too happy to do," and before dinner Tennyson took up Allingham's book of poems and read some of them aloud, to his great delight. "The rich, slow solemn chant of his voice glorified the little poems." After dinner Coventry Patmore came in:

> Over our port we talked of grave matters. T. said his belief rested on two things, a 'Chief Intelligence and Immortality.''—'I could not eat my dinner without a belief in immortality. If I didn't believe in that, I'd go down immediately and jump off Richmond Bridge.' Then to me, rather shortly, 'Why do you laugh?' I murmured that there was something ludicrous in the image of his jumping off Richmond Bridge. 'Well' he rejoined, in such a case I'd as soon make a comic end as a tragic.'

Allingham saw a good deal of Tennyson in his later

years and he retained his admiration and reverence for "The Great Man" to the end of his life but he could argue with him when necessary, especially about Ireland, a subject on which Tennyson remained, like most Englishmen of his time, obtuse and ignorant.

After a dinner party at Aldworth, Allingham notes down the following conversation between himself and Tennyson:

T. 'A Russian noble, who spoke English well, said one morning to an English guest, "I've shot two peasants this morning."—"Pardon me, you mean pheasants." "No, indeed, two men—they were insolent and I shot them"'

W.A. 'In Ireland it's the other way.'

T. 'Couldn't they blow up that horrible island with dynamite and carry it off in pieces—a long way off?'

W.A. 'Why did the English go there?'

T. 'Why did the Normans come to England? The Normans came over here and seized the country, and in a hundred years the English had forgotten all about it, and they were all living together on good terms.'

The discussion continues at some length, but Tennyson comes back to his old point and has the last word:

T. 'The Kelts are so utterly unreasonable! The stupid clumsy Englishman—knock him down, kick him under the tail, kick him under the chin, do anything to him, he gets on his legs again and goes on; the Kelt rages and shrieks and tears everything to pieces!'

Once when he was staying with the Tennysons at Farringford for an Easter holiday, Allingham had a brief encounter with Professor Jowett. Jowett was staying at a neighboring house with two Oxford pupils, and he visited the Tennysons every day. One night Allingham walked home with him:

The conversation turned to the subject of *conventionalities,* and I urged how lamentable it was to see men, and, especially, distinguished men, accepting in public, or even actively supporting ideas which they abjured in their own minds. This was my hobby and I rode it at a pace that the Professor was probably little accustomed to, yet he listened and answered not only with patience but apparent interest, and when we arrived at his door invited me, somewhat to my surprise, to come in and continue the conversation, I remember, in a room dimly lighted with one candle. He seemed to agree with me in the main, but argued to the effect that by an open and unguarded non-conformity a man might ruin his career and lose all influence and authority. I said in my usual impulsive style—'Oh, he would find the apparent obstacles to be only shadows on his road.' To which J. replied gently, but with a tone of conviction, 'I fear he would find them very real'.

He is a soft smooth round man with fat soft hands, and a very gentle voice and manner, but with no weakness of will or lack of perseverance. He is extremely cautious, but not in the least cowardly,—can quietly make his way, doubtless, into very hard substances, as some very soft creatures do (speaking without disparagement). J. indeed has publicly shown great frankness, *for an Oxford don,* and will be a reformer *ab intra.*

Allingham had a respect and admiration for Carlyle second only to that he had for Tennyson. He was a frequent visitor at 5 Cheyne Row and he often accompanied Carlyle on his walks in London. He took lodgings in Chelsea in order to be near Carlyle and when, in 1874, he married Helen Paterson, a watercolor painter, they set up house only a few streets away from Cheyne

Row. Mrs. Allingham painted a watercolor portrait of Carlyle in his old age, which is now in the Scottish National Portrait Gallery. Allingham records in the diary a remark made to him by Carlyle's neice:

> Mary tells me that she said to her uncle—'People say Mr. Allingham is to be your Boswell', and he replied, 'Well, let him try it. He's very accurate'.

But Allingham limited his Boswellian role to recording scraps of Carlyle's conversation and details of his behavior. He noticed his frugality and the horror of waste that his Scottish puritan upbringing had bred in him:

> C. picked up a bit of bread in the street and put it on a ledge, blaming such 'waste of food'.

> He often praised Cobbett's *Cottage Economy,* and spoke of a poor woman who took up straw plaiting from it.

It was dangerous to cross a crowded road with Carlyle, who dodged dashing carriages. ("He may catch his death thus, for he usually insists on crossing when he had made up his mind to it, carrying his stick so as to poke it into a horse's nose at need").

Although he deeply loved and respected, indeed revered Carlyle, Allingham was shrewdly aware of his rockiness and obtuseness. On certain subjects, such as poetry and painting and Ireland, he knew it was useless to argue with Carlyle, though sometimes he could not help it. For all his respect Allingham was no "yes-man". Mr. J. Reade tells a story of a long tirade by Carlyle against Gladstone for a certain Irish measure he had just introduced, when he was walking with Allingham and another friend:

When he finally came to a stop Allingham suggested mildly that perhaps, there might be another side to the question. With a look of disgust Carlyle strode on in front, leaving the two others to follow. When he reached his own door he opened it, turned round and said: "William Allingham, of all the pig-headed, obstinate, cross-grained, argumentative Irishmen in London, you are the worst", after which he slammed the door.

When Carlyle died Allingham paid a brief visit to the room where he lay dead.

I looked upon the honoured face, thin, with hoary hair and beard; the face of a weary Pilgrim, at the end of a long journey, arrived and at rest. The large beautiful eyelids were closed for ever on a pair of eyes that, whether for carrying messages inwards or outwards, had scarce met their equals on earth or left such behind.

Helen made two pencil sketches. As we sat in the parlour the street-door bell rang, and a 'Messenger from the Queen' was said to be in the passage, I went out at Mary's request and found a Scotchman of middle age, who said he was 'sent by the Queen to enquire after Mr. Carlyle'; I told him of the death. . .

A walk as in a dream. How strange all the moving crowds, all the busy trivialities going on! No change felt on earth or in air. I thought, looking at this stranger and that, 'if I said to you "Carlyle is dead," would you care?'

With Rossetti and the Pre-Raphaelite circle Allingham found himself among his contemporaries. There is a cheerful buoyancy in his accounts of his days and evenings with "D.G.R.":

Monday, June 27 [1864] Got down to Chelsea by half-past-eight to D.G.R.'s. Breakfasted in a small lofty room on first floor with window looking onto the garden. Fanny in white. Then we went into the garden and lay on the grass, eating strawberries and looking at the peacock. F. went to look at the 'chicking', her plural of chicken. Then Swinburne came in. . .and after him Whistler.

Monday, 14 October [1867] Evening, with D.G.R. to Ned's [Edward Burne-Jones]. R. lolls and runs down Raffael, Ned and Webb remonstrate. No music. R. and I walking back take wrong turn—'This is bl -y! He very fond of this expletive - as well as other phrases (F. sometimes says, 'Rizetti, I shall leave the room! - I'll put you out in the scullery!' etc.) Lounging chat till 1 or 2, with rusks and sherry.

Rossetti and Allingham remained friendly for many years. According to Violet Hunt, who had access to Allingham's papers, it was he who first discovered Elizabeth Siddal in a milliner's shop and introduced her to the P.R.B. Allingham made detailed criticisms and corrections of Rossetti's manuscript poems and Ruskin said that he could only ink in Allingham's pencil. Rossetti kept up a correspondence with Allingham for many years, but in the end the two friends drifted apart; their attitudes to life were markedly different. In his life of Rossetti, Oswald Doughty speaks of 'the unbridgeable gulf between the disillusioned, cynical, reclusive widower and the sheltered, sentimental, aging bachelor.''

When Allingham moved to Lymington he frequently pressed Rossetti to come down and join him for a holiday. Rossetti hesitated and put it off several times, and when finally he came in September, 1867, the visit was not a success. When they take a walk,

R. walks very characteristically, with a peculiar lounging gait, often trailing the point of his umbrella on the ground, but still obstinately pushing on and making way. . .Then suddenly he will fling himself down somewhere, and refuse to stir an inch further. His favourite attitude - on his back, one knee raised, hands behind head. On a sofa he often too, curls himself up like a cat. He very seldom takes particular

notice of anything as he goes, and cares nothing about natural history, or science in any form or degree. It is plain
that the simple, the natural, the naive: are merely insipid in
his mouth; he must have strong savours, in art, in literature
and in life. . .He cannot endure Wordsworth, any more than
I can S. [Swinburne]

Rossetti mocked his friend's pious attitude to the
memory of the great. Allingham would cherish a violet
from the grave of Shelley. Once when he was at the
barber's with Carlyle, he picked up and pocketed a lock
of the old man's hair. He plucked some grasses from a
field once ploughed by Burns, and Rossetti exclaimed:

Fancy carying about grasses for hours and days from a field
where Burns ploughed up a daisy! Good God, if I found the
daisy itself there, I would sooner swallow it than be
troubled to carry it twenty yards.

The interest of Allingham's diary is not solely due to
his acquaintance with literary personalities. Allingham
talked to the humble as well as the famous. He has
many chance encounters with people on his walks. He
had a warm humanity and did what he could to help
those in trouble. On one occasion he met a poor-looking
woman who had walked all the way from London to
Portland to visit her son who was in the convict prison
for theft. She had seen him "in a cage as you might say"
for about half-an-hour, and now she was walking back
to London. Allingham, moved bv her story, gave her
some money, for which she was very grateful. He notes
in his diary: "What women suffer from husbands, and
from children!" Although the diary is a personal one it
is not primarily confessional, and Allingham does not
elaborate on his own feelings, but of course they
emerge. We get brief glimpses of his loneliness ("Has

anybody walked habitually alone as much as I?") and his longing for marriage and family life. Allingham can hardly be counted one of the great English diarists, but the diary is full of interest and it is eminently readable. Had he never written a line of poetry, the diary would still entitle him to a modest place in the annals of literature.

Allingham was by nature a rambler and a literary pilgrim. When he first came to London as a boy of eighteen, he roamed the streets with eager curiosity and went to stare with awe and reverence at a brass plate inscribed CHARLES DICKENS. In his forties he walked through many parts of England, Scotland, and Wales and even made an expedition to France. Rossetti, half-admiring, half-scornful, wrote to his friend William Bell Scott, at a time when Allingham was rambling through the Burns country: "Nothing but the most absolute calm and enjoyment of outside nature could account for so much gadding hither and thither on the soles of his two feet."

Allingham was by no means always in a state of "absolute calm", but he did certainly enjoy outside nature; he also enjoyed observing people and their different manners and ways of life. From 1867 onwards he contributed twenty travelogues to *Fraser's* magazine, and in 1873 he published *Rambles* by Patricius Walker. When *Varieties in Prose* was published after his death the first two volumes were given to these rambles.

As a travel-writer Allingham is quiet but effective. He succeeds in conveying to us the feel of the places he visits; he gives us not only accurate description of landscape and buildings, but his own reactions to scene and event, and the personal reflections that arise on his rambles. The reader shares with him "the harvest of a quiet eye." This was a favorite phrase with Allingham and it accurately describes his usual mood as a traveler. But of course his impressions are by no means always those of gentle enjoyment. His quiet prose is enlivened by flashes of humour and irony. On one occasion when he was walking in the Wye Valley his view of a famous stretch of landscape was hopelessly obstructed by a huge blank wall enclosing a private domain. He could not get permission to walk through the park, so he "relieved" his "feelings a little by composing an epitaph.:

'Here lies, etc, etc, whose most memorable action was to build a very long and high stone wall on the banks of the Wye, near Chepstow, shutting out as far as possible, the human race from the enjoyment of an extensive and beautiful landscape.' "

He attended the Scott Centenary Festival in Edinburgh and his account of it is quietly deflating:

Some American newspapers published (by telegraph) most flaming accounts of the Festival—flags, flowers, bells, illuminations, multitudes, notabilities, enthusiasm. To one who assisted at the actual thing it seemed rather a flat affair. The Festival (tickets, one pound each) was in the Corn Exchange, Grassmarket, a large area, decorated with blue and red calico and gaudy banners, in the style of an infant-school feast. Two thousand people were said to be present, and to most of them the speeches were inaudible. . .The creature comforts consisted of wine (claret and sherry) and fruit; and of the former a good share must have gone to the waiters, judging from the appearances in my part of the house towards the end of the proceedings. One waiter had seated himself in an open hamper full of wine glasses. Another, when I spoke to him, was unable to give any articulate answer, but smiled in a friendly way and patted

me on the shoulder, to express his good-will. He for one
seemed to enjoy the Festival.

Although Allingham enjoyed the creature comforts of
a friendly inn with good food and wine, he was an ad-
venturous traveler and prepared to take chances. When
he found the Trossachs hotel full up, he went off to a
cottage where Gaelic was spoken. He slept in a box-bed
in a small room with a low ceiling and the window
nailed up so that he was obliged to leave the door into
the kitchen open, "half smoke being better than no air."
But he enjoyed his breakfast next morning:

> I had a capital breakfast, better tea then I ever got in an
> English hotel and two new-laid eggs boiled to perfection.
> While I ate them, the hen ran about the floor picking up the
> crumbs, which was only fair. Jam was not wanting; and
> there was cheese, which in agreement with Mr. Boswell, 'I
> cannot help disliking at breakfast'. He adds, 'It is the cus-
> tom over all the Highlands to have it.'

In Normandy he joined a Catholic procession to Mont
St. Michel with everyone carrying tapers and singing. He
alone was taperless and silent, feeling himself very much
a Protestant, but the Church soon got the better of him.
A polite ecclesiastic supplied him with a taper and a
neighbour gave him a light, "and there I was 'counted
in' as the Americans say."

He did not confine himself to well-known tourist
areas and literary shrines; he even made an expedition to
Margate, in search of cool air:

> Cockney, prosaic, vulgar in the direst degree, of course, but
> fresh and cool. I took the train and slept that night in
> Margate. Fresh air I found; and also two of the most roman-
> tic particulars I have met in any English place: first, a din-
> ing-room where they were catching fish for dinner out of
> the window; second, a man whose profession it seemed to

be to recite from memory classical English poetry in the open air. He was giving *To be or not to be,* as I passed along the sea-terrace by star-light, and followed it with *Alexander's Feast.*

The rambles of Patricius Walker could hardly be called exciting; he had no amorous adventures and he never fell among thieves. He did not travel as Cobbett did with a passionate belief in social change. He was the polite Victorian gentleman traveler, humble, as befits a walker, but a shrewd and keen observer.

Although he took the Christian name of Patricius, the Walker of these rambles is an Englishman rather than an Irishman. "My country is the United Kingdom," he remarks in parenthesis, and apart from an occasional reference to Irish scenes and Irish customs, there is nothing to suggest that he travels as an Irishman. He had already settled himself in England for a number of years and had become increasingly an Englishman, with London as his literary and geographical center.

Allingham is often at his best in brief reflective notes and jottings. He contributed a series of "Ivy-leaves" to *Fraser's,* which purported to come from the Hermitage, Epping Forest, and were signed "Eastern Hermit". His mode of expressing himself tends to epigram and aphorism, and what he has to say is frequently worth pondering:

> In highly cultured society nothing is allowed to interrupt conversation; in other society anything and everything. This is a good test of the degree of general culture in any circle.

> Of two kinds of relation to society I have always had a dread—of being disreputable, and of being 'respectable'. They are equally against good taste, and equally inconvenient.

At the time of his death he was collecting a series of paragraphs and notes on various subjects under the title *By the Way*. His wife published them in 1912 under this title, together with a number of verses and fragments. Not all his reflections are interesting, and naturally he repeats himself a good deal, but these notes too, amongst many platitudes contain some apt and pithily expressed comments on the life and books that Allingham knew. Here a few samples:

> British cooking is unimaginative. I have dined for three months in my lodging, and eaten ninety successive mutton chops.

> Vanity is the most cleverly versatile of the passions. A man can manage to be proud of anything, of any defect; any fault; any vice, almost any failure or any crime.

> One unaccustomed to the exercise is apt to find reading Carlyle like riding a dromedary—you are borne powerfully along, but dreadfully jolted and jumbled, and your carrier grumbles and growls all through the journey.

6

An Irish Victorian

Although Allingham left Ireland in 1863 he still continued to think of Ireland and Irish affairs as his subject. In 1865 he made a serious attempt to get his literary pension increased so that he might leave the Customs and devote himself to "a deliberate study of Ireland— historical, topographical and social." He talked over this "scheme or dream" of his with Woolner, who encouraged it. Woolner spoke about the matter to Tennyson, who took it up with great good will and mentioned it to Gladstone. Allingham also wrote to Carlyle and to Browning. Carlyle was discouraging; he was all for Allingham working at a History of Ireland and repeated his admiration for an historical introduction that Allingham had written for the *Ballyshannon Almanac* in 1862, but he didn't approve of his pulling up his tether again. Browning was more sympathetic; he passed on the letter he had received from Allingham to Gladstone with a covering letter of his own commending Allingham to the Chancellor of the Exchequer:

I have found Mr. Allingham admirably conscientious, full of industry, energetic yet self-controlling, and only ambitious in a noble way. His poetical productions are in evidence enough, and nobody respects them more than I.

Allingham's hope was that his pension might be increased by an amount equivalent to his salary from the Customs, to give him £150 in all, so that he would be free to read and write, visit libraries and study records. He felt that his background and long residence in Ireland, together with his detachment from parties, made him a suitable person to embark on Irish history.

But nothing came of Allingham's dream. No increase of pension was forthcoming from the Treasury, so he remained at his Customs post until 1870, when he was appointed sub-editor of *Fraser's* magazine. In 1874 he became editor; in the same year he married Helen Paterson, an English watercolor painter, and the rest of his life was spent in or near London. He died in Hampstead in 1889, and after his death he was cremated by his own special wish (cremation was still a radical novelty in England), and his ashes were then taken back to Ballyshannon and buried alongside many other Allinghams in St. Anne's churchyard. At the end the Irish link was re-established.

Allingham never wrote his projected History of Ireland, though he did write one or two articles for *Fraser's,* and the last phase of his life became essentially an English one. Yet he belongs to an Irish tradition. He is not in the same category as Davis, Mangan, and Ferguson, for all the enthusiasm of Yeats and Katharine Tynan. I mean by this, not that he is a lesser poet—at his best Allingham goes beyond all three of the "holy trinity"—but that he is less fully involved with the search for an Irish identity. Not only did he leave Ireland, but his eyes were early turned toward English and American models; he read English and American magazines, Leigh Hunt's *London Journal* and *The Dial.* Had he lived in Dublin, as the members of the "holy trinity" did, things might have been different, but in Ballyshannon there was not even a bookshop, let alone anyone interested in Irish literature.

He did send a poem or two to the *Dublin University Magazine* and he made the acquaintance of William Carleton. Had Carleton been more encouraging the connection with Dublin might have been strengthened, but after Allingham had written him a rather tactless letter Carleton must have snubbed him. Allingham replied apologetically but we hear no more of the connection, and London altogether replaced Dublin as the center of Allingham's literary world. His stars were Leigh Hunt, Tennyson, Carlyle, (Emerson in America), and his friends became the young Pre-Raphaelites.

Unfortunately the prevailing mood in Victorian poetry steered Allingham away from the untapped Irish sources that lay around him toward the world of daydream and ideal Beauty. There is an aspect of Victorian poetry that is neatly pinpointed in James Joyce's description of the poet-laureate, "Lawn-Tennyson, gentleman-poet." This suggests a well-mown smooth surface, a civilized literary decorum befitting a Victorian country residence, an avoidance of the seamier sides of life that we find in Villon and in Synge, for example. Synge, as Yeats put it, loved "all that has edge, all that is salt in the mouth, all that is rough to the hand, all that heightens the emotions by contest, all that stings into life the sense of tragedy." Synge was to find his material on the Arans, on a seacoast similar to the coast of Donegal.

If Yeats had come before instead of after Allingham he might have given him the advice he gave Synge, when he sent him to the Arans: "Express a life that has never found expression." Allingham was aware of this local life, as his letters and diary show. He was much in demand as a letter writer and reader by the poor people of Ballyshannon, who were, of course, mostly illiterate. So he came to know a good deal about their lives and fortunes and their human relationships. In a letter to the Brownings, written in September 1853, we have an example of the kind of human situation that he was drawn into in his role of letter writer:

> There is in this place a marvel relating to drownings which was talked of recently, though I could not trace it to anyone who called himself a witness. The recent occasion was this, a man and a boy were fishing on the sea-rocks; the boy, striving to cross a chasm, fell in; the man leaped in to save him; they grappled and both were lost. On the night before (said the people then) a great human multitude of old and young had been seen, or at least heard, passing along the road on which these two lived—coming from the sea and again returning towards it. Probably, the Drowned seeking or bringing message for the next of doom. There was something more than commonly touching about the boy's fate. His body was found on the day your letter came, which somehow makes me think I ought to tell you of it. A rough road brought me (the letter in my pocket) to the sea-side, where there are high crags, with ruins of a castle, and under them black, shelving rocks, cloven into deep fissures, where the two were drowned. The surge was spilt along, hissing like new milk, but today seeming much less innocent. In front of a cottage they were staunching with tar the seams of a rough coffin. The boy's father has been for years in America. In June of this year he wrote to the uncle with money, desiring him to come out and bring

"Francis", now about sixteen years old, along with him. The letter, which I read, after giving particular directions for the journey, says "I am proud to tell you it is my second son, only six years old, that is writing this," and in a postscript the second son writes from himself, "I send a kiss for my brother Francis, and I'll give him two more when he comes here." The letter came in the interval between the drowning of the boy and the finding of his corpse. I remember a little point of another sort in the affair. The money was in care of the Priest, who properly refused to give it up till the father should be told what had happened. The uncle came to me to write—he wished the father to be persuaded to leave the money for him, "Soap him up, Sir," says he, "as well as you can." This was not hardness, only want of dexterity in phrasing. Perhaps there is oftener difference between people in phrase than in feeling.

There is surely the raw material here for a poem or a short story. Even as it stands the passage would make part of a journal like *The Aran Islands.* When Allingham was pondering some kind of prose work, 'to introduce bits of characters, humor, scenery, etc., it is a pity that there was no friend to advise him to write a personal journal of life in the North West of Ireland. He could certainly have done such a book as well as W.R. Trench, the land agent, whose *Realities of Irish Life* (1868) is full of interest. Allingham's book would have been very different, but perhaps even more interesting.

It was not to be. Allingham was too much the Victorian gentleman, shrinking a little from what was coarse and rough to the hand. Synge, although born into the gentleman class, had a natural leaning towards the world of peasants and tramps. According to George Moore he disliked the orderly life of his mother's house and preferred the cottages and cabins where he could lie in bed smoking shag and talking to a peasant. Though Allingham did frequent fairs and assidously visited cottages and cabins, he preferred the refined world of the London drawing room and the artist's studio. His natural inclination was strongly encouraged by prevailing Victorian taste and sentiment, and so we get dainty poems about flowers and fairies, instead of the coarse realitites of Irish life; sugar instead of salt.

But even if much of Allingham's work is too polite and sweet for modern taste, and even though he leaned away from Irish reality toward the Ideal and the Beautiful and the Good, there still remains a sufficient body of his work rooted in the Ireland he knew to give him an honorable place in the Irish tradition. There is *Laurence Bloomfield* for a start, which is far more deeply rooted in Ireland than *The Deserted Village* and is a finer poem into the bargain, for all its longeurs and other weaknesses. Then there are the ballads and songs, some parts of his diary and letters,—all these entitle him to be counted among the Irish writers.

Allingham sincerely wished his name as a poet to be connected with Ireland. Writing to Samuel Ferguson in June, 1885, he said:

> When you come into my mind (which is very often, my dear Ferguson) the thought is apt to rise that hereafter, perhaps, they will be reckoned among the friends of Ireland who have done something, each in his degree, to make her name interesting and amiable in the ear of mankind.

Apart from *Laurence Bloomfield* and other poems, Allingham did much to counter the ignorance and prejudice of Victorian Englishmen against Ireland. His articles in *Fraser's* on Irish history and Irish place names were deliberate attempts to reduce the barriers. He begins an account of an Irish legend in *Fraser's* (May, 1875) with a statement of the general English attitude to Ireland:

> Early Irish History is to the English reader, extremely unin-
> teresting—nay, exasperating. Uncouth names, unknown
> people, unintelligible events, meet him at every turn; the
> associations raised in his mind by a recognisable phrase here
> and there, such as 'Fenian', are the contrary of pleasant;
> indeed the words 'Ireland' and 'Irish' themselves suggest
> discord, complaint, beggary, boasting, and all kinds of both-
> eration. 'No Irish need apply'.

To counter this English prejudice he endeavored to approach Irish history and literature in "a calm, deliberate,
impartial spirit." If only Gladstone had agreed to raise
his pension Allingham might have given us a useful history of Ireland.

W.B. Yeats and Katharine Tynan, in their eagerness to
promote an Irish tradition in literature, have perhaps
over-emphasized the Irishness of Allingham's poetry;
but on the other hand he has been unfairly neglected by
most other Irish critics, and he is little known to Irish
readers. Allingham had no faith in Home Rule for Ireland, and he believed the Irish language was only an
obstruction to real progress, but he had deep feeling for
Ireland and her people, so that in the final balance he
must clearly be reckoned "True brother of a company/
That sang, to sweeten Ireland's wrong. . . ."

Finally, if we look beyond Ireland, to the English-
speaking world, is there a place for Allingham in the
annals of English literature? I think there is certainly a
modest place. If we consider the critical attention that
has been paid to some of Allingham's contemporaries
and friends—Patmore and Clough for example—it must
be agreed that Allingham has been unfairly neglected.
Many English critics, Saintsbury, Gosse and Garnett—

were hostile or cold. Even Geoffrey Grigson, who introduced the *Diary* when it was reprinted in 1967, is condescending and lukewarm. Apart from *Laurence Bloomfield*, he finds only two poems to commend and one of these is 'The Fairies'. He sees Allingham as something of an intruder into London literary circles. "Again and again there is more than a hint of patronizing—or suffering—this large, long-nosed, dark-haired, not so very well-educated 'Englishman' from outer Ireland." Grigson is mistaken about the general attitude of Allingham's friends toward him, as he is about his physical size (he was slight in figure), but discussion of this would take us into biographical rather than critical considerations.

Allingham is not a poet who makes a sharp impact on readers. He did not impress himself on his own times and his circle of readers was small. He has none of the linguistic originality and genius of Hopkins. His life was not dramatic like that of Francis Thompson or Ernest Dowson. There is no abandonment to religious or aesthetic or erotic passion in his life or his poetry. His verse is strongly traditional and his language followed, sometimes too closely, the path of literary convention. He believed that poetry should delight the ear and for this reason he considered Browning a heretic and Whitman no poet. But for all his limitations and his Victorian primness, he has left us some portion of "memorable speech", and his quiet unassuming qualities as a writer and a man grow on the reader as familiarity increases. In addition to *Laurence Bloomfield* there are two or three dozen other poems—ballads, songs, and personal or descriptive poems and some piquant "blackberries" worth preserving. How many minor poets give us more? In addition there is the diary, the letters and rambles, and some thought-provoking reflections by the way. Enough surely to gain admission to the lower slopes of Parnassus.

When Allingham visited Penzance in Cornwall he noticed the statue of Sir Humphrey Davy, a native of the town with his "Davy Lamp" beside him and he meditated: "Better worth while methought (if such things be worth while), to have a statue in the street of one's own town, close by your birthplace and grammar school, than to find elbowroom in the monumental miscellany of the cold aisles of Westminster." There is a bronze head of William Allingham outside the bank in Ballyshannon, where he once worked as a clerk. In the "Bank House" next door, his father's residence as bank manager, the young William scratched his name and an imperfectly rhymed couplet on the glass of his bedroom window, perhaps the window from which he saw the inviting gleam of that mysterious water which he never found. The couplet runs:

> This name's duration shall outlast
> The hand that wrote it on the glass

The hand that wrote it has long since gone, but the name is not yet forgotten.

Selected Bibliography

The Works

Poems. London: Chapman and Hall, 1850.
Day and Night Songs. London: Routledge and Co., 1854.
The Music Master and Two Series of Day and Night Songs. Routledge and Co., 1855.
Laurence Bloomfield in Ireland. London: Macmillan and Co., 1864. Reprint, 1972.
Fifty Modern Poems. London: Bell and Daldy, 1865. Reprint, 1973.
Rambles, by Patricius Walker. London: Longmans, 1873.
Songs, Ballads and Stories. London: Bell and Sons, 1877.
Evil May-Day. London: David Stott, 1882.
Ashby Manor. (A play in two acts) London: David Stott, 1883.
Blackberries. London: G. Phillip and Son, 1884.

A uniform collected edition in six volumes of all the poems variously rearranged was published in London by Reeves and Turner as follows:

1	*Irish Songs and Poems*	1887
2	*Flower Pieces*	1888
3	*Life and Phantasy*	1889
4	*Laurence Bloomfield in Ireland*	1890
5	*Thought and Word* and *Ashby Manor*	1890
6	*Blackberries*	1890

A Diary. Edited by H. Allingham and D. Radford, London: Macmillan, 1907.

By the Way. (Verses, fragments and notes). Edited by Helen Allingham. London: Longmans, Green and Co., 1912.

Later Selections:

Sixteen Poems. Edited by W.B. Yeats. Dublin: Dun Emer Press, 1905.

Poems by William Allingham, selected and arranged by Helen Allingham. London: Macmillan 1912 (Golden Treasury Series)

The Poems of William Allingham. Edited with an introduction by John Hewitt. Dublin: The Dolmen Press, 1967.

Letters

Allingham's letters are widely scattered and only a few of them have appeared in print. Some of them, to Leigh Hunt, to Arthur Hughes, and to Emerson, were published by his widow in a collection mainly consisting of letters written to him by his friends (*Letters to William Allingham,* ed. H. Allingham and E. Baumer Williams, Longmans, 1911). Not long after this book was published a supplement was printed containing letters from Allingham to Mr. and Mrs. Browning, which were acquired at a Browning Sale in May 1913. A few others have appeared in memoirs of his friends such as Patmore, Woolner, and Ferguson. A considerable number, including forty-six letters to Henry Sutton, remain unpublished.

Bibliographies

O'Hegarty, P.S. *A Bibliography of William Allingham.* Dublin. Privately printed by Alex. Thom and Co. Ltd., 1945.
Warner, Alan. "William Allingham: A Bibliographical Survey." *Irish Booklore,* 2, no. 2 (1975).

Biographies

No biography has yet been published, but some biographical information may be found in the following books:

Hill, G.B., ed. *The Letters of Rossetti to Allingham.*

Allingham, H. and Williams, E. Baumer, eds. *Letters to William Allingham*. London: Longmans, Green and Co., 1911. Reprint, 1971.

Warner, Alan. *William Allingham: an Introduction.* Dublin: The Dolmen Press, 1971.

Selected Critical Studies

Yeats, W.B. "A Poet we have Neglected" (Review of Allingham's collected poems). *United Ireland* (12 Dec., 1891).

Yeats, W.B. "William Allingham (1824-1889)." Introductory sketch contributed to Alfred Miles' anthology *The Poets and Poetry of the Century.* London, 1892.

Note: both the above articles are reprinted in *Uncollected Prose by W.B. Yeats,* vol. I, ed. Frayne, John P., London: Macmillan, 1970.

Johnson, Lionel. "William Allingham." Introductory sketch contributed to *A Treasury of Irish Poetry in the English Tongue*. Edited by Brooke and Rolleston. London: Smith, Elder and Co., 1900.

Drinkwater, John. "The Poetry of William Allingham." *The New Ireland Review* (Feb. 1909).

Kropf, Hans. *William Allingham Und Seine Dichtung.* Bern Univ., Dec. 1925.

Taylor, Geoffrey. "Willliam Allingham." *The Bell* (May 1942).

MacDonogh, Patrick. *"Laurence Bloomfield in Ireland."* *The Dublin Magazine* (Jan.-March 1950).

Evans, Ifor. *English Poetry in the Later Nineteenth Century.* London: Methuen. 2nd ed., London: Methuen, 1966, pp. 132-36.

Hewitt, John. Introduction to *The Poems of William Allingham.* Edited by Hewitt. Dublin: The Dolmen Press, 1967.

Warner, Alan. *"William Allingham: A Victorian Boswell?"* *The Dublin Magazine* (Summer 1967).

McMahon, Sean. "The Boy from his Bedroom Window." *Eire-Ireland* (Summer 1970).